Cor...

1,000 BIBLE Q&As

Test Your Bible Knowledge

BARBOUR
PUBLISHING

Published by Barbour Publishing, Inc., 1810 Barbour Drive, Uhrichsville, Ohio 44683, www.barbourbooks.com

Our mission is to inspire the world with the life-changing message of the Bible.

Printed in the United States of America.

CONTENTS

SO YOU THINK YOU KNOW THE BIBLE?

Okay, prove it!

The Bible's a big, serious book—but it's also full of fun and fascinating detail lending itself to trivia quizzes. So here's a brand-new collection of 1,000 questions, divided into 100 categories, designed to see just what you remember from God's Word.

How's your knowledge of. . .

- All Creatures, Great and Small (animals of the Bible)

- Days of Creation (the origins account of Genesis 1–2)

- Getting from Here to There (biblical transportation)

- Lies and Consequences (the disasters of dishonesty)

- People to See (beautiful Bible folks)

- Places to Be (important scriptural locales)

- "Z" People (names that begin with the alphabet's final letter)

. . .and dozens of other topics? You'll find out here!

Some categories are truly trivial, and just for fun—while others share important details about scripture,

God, and Christian living. A variety of question types—open-ended, multiple choice, and "true or trick"—will challenge without overwhelming you with minutiae.

1,000 Bible Q and As is ideal for Sunday schools, small groups, family game nights, or personal reading, for readers from junior high and up.

Note: Answers begin on page 209.

Quiz 1
"A" PEOPLE

The Bible is filled with all types of characters. Here are some less familiar people whose names all start with "A." Do you know them?

1. MULTIPLE CHOICE: Achan deliberately sinned by
    a. refusing to go to battle
    b. blaspheming God
    c. speaking out against Joshua
    d. stealing things devoted to God

2. TRUE OR TRICK: Abigail was King Saul's wife.

3. QUOTE IT: 2 Samuel 18:9 says Absalom's "head caught hold of the oak, and he was. . ."

4. MULTIPLE CHOICE: Abednego's Hebrew name was
    a. Hananiah
    b. Mishael
    c. Azariah
    d. Hadassah

5. TRUE OR TRICK: Asa was one of the good kings of Judah.

6. TRUE OR TRICK: Abner was captain of David's army.

7. TRUE OR TRICK: Annas was a high priest at the same time as Caiaphas.

8. MULTIPLE CHOICE: Eighty-four-year-old Anna was
   a. a prophetess
   b. from the tribe of Asher
   c. a widow
   d. all of the above

9. MULTIPLE CHOICE: Agabus was
   a. a prophet
   b. a king
   c. a priest
   d. a shepherd

10. QUOTE IT: 1 Kings 16:30 says Ahab "did evil in the sight of the LORD. . ."

Quiz 2
ABUNDANCE

The Bible contains many promises of blessings to those that follow God. Here are some of them.

1. QUOTE IT: Psalm 23:6 says, "Surely goodness and mercy shall. . ."

2. QUOTE IT: "Give, and it shall be given unto you; good measure, pressed down, and shaken together, and. . ."

3. MULTIPLE CHOICE: "The blessing of the LORD, it maketh. . ."
   a. rich
   b. wise
   c. courageous
   d. love

4. QUOTE IT: "Blessed are the meek. . ."

5. FILL IN THE BLANK: "Ask and it shall be _____ you; seek, and ye shall _____; knock, and it shall be _____ unto you."

6. MULTIPLE CHOICE: The first blessing in the Bible was pronounced upon
    a. Adam and Eve
    b. sea creatures and birds
    c. Abel
    d. the earth

7. MULTIPLE CHOICE: Of what king does 2 Chronicles 17:4–5 say the Lord gave riches and honor in abundance because he walked in God's commandments?
    a. Solomon
    b. Hezekiah
    c. Jehoshaphat
    d. Josiah

8. FILL IN THE BLANK: Revelation 2:7 says that to the person who overcomes, God will let him eat of the tree of _____.

9. TRUE OR TRICK: Proverbs 10:6 says that blessings are upon the heart of the just.

10. MULTIPLE CHOICE: According to Ephesians 1:3, where are all spiritual blessings?
    a. in our hearts
    b. in the church
    c. in heavenly places in Christ
    d. in God's hands

Quiz 3
ALL CREATURES, GREAT AND SMALL

Throughout the Bible, all types of animals play important roles. But these animals certainly were not pets. How much do you know about them?

1. TRUE OR TRICK: God named all the animals.

2. FILL IN THE BLANK: David boasted of killing a _____ and a _____.

3. MULTIPLE CHOICE: Which of the following people is *not* associated with a dove?
    a. Noah
    b. Jesus
    c. Jonah
    d. Moses

4. QUOTE IT: Jesus said it was easier for a camel to go through the eye of a needle than. . .

5. MULTIPLE CHOICE: When Balaam beat his donkey and the animal spoke to him, what did it say?

    a. "Can't you see the angel?"

    b. "Have I been in the habit of doing this to you?"

    c. "You need to obey the Lord."

    d. "You can't go curse Israel."

6. MULTIPLE CHOICE: Which of the following animals did God tell the Israelites was unclean—and they were not allowed to eat it?

    a. sheep

    b. cattle

    c. grasshoppers

    d. camels

7. QUOTE IT: Peter said Christ was a lamb without blemish. . .

8. TRUE OR TRICK: When God brought the plague of frogs upon Egypt, the Egyptian magicians brought up more frogs.

9. TRUE OR TRICK: Unicorns are mentioned in the Bible.

10. FILL IN THE BLANK: According to Proverbs 30:30, there is no animal stronger than a _____.

Quiz 4
ANGELS AMONG US

Angels don't really look the way they are portrayed in paintings. The Bible describes them quite differently. Do you recognize these descriptions?

1. TRUE OR TRICK: Seraphim have six wings.

2. QUOTE IT: In Daniel 10:13, Daniel calls Michael. . .

3. MULTIPLE CHOICE: The number of angels mentioned by name in the Bible is
    a. two
    b. three
    c. four
    d. seven

4. TRUE OR TRICK: Psalm 78:24–25 says manna is angel's food.

5. MULTIPLE CHOICE: The apostle Paul's description "an angel of light" refers to
    a. another apostle
    b. the angel of the Lord
    c. the angel who stopped Abraham from
       sacrificing Isaac
    d. Satan

6. MULTIPLE CHOICE: Which of the following did *not* see a host of angels?

    a. Jacob

    b. Peter

    c. shepherds at Bethlehem

    d. Elisha

7. QUOTE IT: In Revelation 10:6, John saw an angel lift his hand to heaven and declare. . .

8. FILL IN THE BLANK: _____ was a devout Gentile in Caesarea who saw an angel.

9. MULTIPLE CHOICE: The angels have charge over the righteous to do what?

    a. keep them in all their ways

    b. bear them up in their hands

    c. make them wise

    d. a and b

10. FILL IN THE BLANK: 1 Corinthians 6:3 says _____ will judge the angels.

Quiz 5
BABIES BORN

The most famous baby of all time whose birth was foretold was, of course, Jesus. What great wonder and joy His birth caused! But Jesus was not the only baby whose parents greatly anticipated the birth. What do you know about these babies and their parents?

1. QUOTE IT: The Lord told Rebekah that two nations...

2. FILL IN THE BLANK: _____ name means "laughter" because his elderly mother, Sarah, laughed when she was told she was going to have a son.

3. MULTIPLE CHOICE: Mahershalalhashbaz was the son promised to
    a. Isaiah
    b. Elijah
    c. Ezekiel
    d. Jeremiah

4. FILL IN THE BLANK: Hannah's son whom she promised to dedicate to the Lord was _____.

5. TRUE OR TRICK: An angel told Zacharias that he was going to have a son to be called John.

6. TRUE OR TRICK: Moses' parents were from the tribe of Judah.

7. MULTIPLE CHOICE: The unusual thing about the prophet Hosea's children was
    a. they were triplets
    b. they weren't his
    c. their mother was a prostitute
    d. they were all named Hosea

8. TRUE OR TRICK: The angel of the Lord told Samson's father that Samson was to be a Nazarite from the day he was born.

9. MULTIPLE CHOICE: Ruth and Boaz's son, Obed, was given his name by
    a. an angel
    b. his father
    c. Naomi
    d. neighbors

10. TRUE OR TRICK: The Shunammite woman's son died and was brought back to life by Elijah.

Quiz 6
BORN AGAIN

Being born again was a confusing concept to early Christians, yet they believed. What do you know about being born again?

1. FILL IN THE BLANK: Paul was struck blind by the light when he met Jesus on the road to _____.

2. QUOTE IT: The apostle Paul wrote to Timothy that God saves us "by the washing of. . ."

3. QUOTE IT: When Paul and Silas were freed from prison by an earthquake, the jailer asked them, "Sirs. . ."

4. MULTIPLE CHOICE: When Philip explained salvation to the Ethiopian eunuch, the eunuch
   a. wanted to be baptized
   b. went on his way unmoved
   c. went back to Jerusalem
   d. told Philip he had to think about it

5. QUOTE IT: When Jesus told Nicodemus he must be born again, Nicodemus replied, "Can a man enter a second time. . ."

6. TRUE OR TRICK: Cornelius was the first Gentile to become a Christian.

7. TRUE OR TRICK: When Paul preached to Agrippa, the king said, "You persuaded me to be a Christian."

8. MULTIPLE CHOICE: Lydia welcomed Paul into her home and was baptized. Lydia was a seller of
   a. wheat
   b. robes
   c. wares
   d. purple

9. MULTIPLE CHOICE: When Peter preached on Pentecost, how many were baptized?
   a. a thousand
   b. two thousand
   c. three thousand
   d. twenty thousand

10. MULTIPLE CHOICE: Simon, the sorcerer in Samaria who was born again, was later rebuked by Peter because
   a. Simon recanted
   b. Simon told everyone he was an apostle
   c. Simon tried to buy the gift of the Holy Spirit
   d. Simon preached his own gospel

Quiz 7
BROTHERLY LOVE

Jesus said whoever does the will of God is His (and our) brother, sister, and mother. What do you know about brotherly love?

1. FILL IN THE BLANK: Hebrews 13:1 says, "Let brotherly love _____."

2. MULTIPLE CHOICE: Othniel, the first judge of Israel, was the younger brother of
    a. Moses and Aaron
    b. Joshua
    c. Caleb
    d. Boaz

3. TRUE OR TRICK: Moses was older than Aaron.

4. FILL IN THE BLANK: 2 Peter 1:7 says we are to add brotherly kindness to our godliness, and to our brotherly kindness _____.

5. FILL IN THE BLANKS: Love _____ all things, _____ all things, _____ all things, _____ all things.

6. MULTIPLE CHOICE: Abraham's brother, who was the father of Lot, was
   a. Haran
   b. Terah
   c. Laban
   d. Milcah

7. FILL IN THE BLANK: Proverbs 17:17 says a friend loveth at all times, and a brother is born for _____.

8. TRUE OR TRICK: Andrew brought his brother Peter to meet Jesus.

9. QUOTE IT: After Jacob died, Joseph's brothers were afraid he would finally turn on them. Instead, Joseph told them, "Ye thought evil against me; but God. . ."

10. TRUE OR TRICK: In addition to his friend, Jonathan, David also had a brother named Jonathan.

Quiz 8
CHARITY CASES

Bible translators use the words *love* and *charity* interchangeably. We are to practice charity by loving others. How well do you know these charity cases?

1. MULTIPLE CHOICE: Dorcas was well known for and loved for her good works, which mainly consisted of
    a. feeding the hungry
    b. sewing garments for the poor
    c. giving money
    d. letting travelers stay in her house

2. TRUE OR TRICK: The man Jesus healed at the pool of Bethesda had been sick for forty years.

3. MULTIPLE CHOICE: In the days of famine, Elijah promised a widow that her flour and oil would not fail if she would
    a. believe in God
    b. believe in Elijah
    c. make Elijah a little cake
    d. give Elijah her son

4. FILL IN THE BLANK: Bartimaeus was a blind _____.

5. TRUE OR TRICK: The king of Babylon, Evilmerodach, took pity on his captive, the king of Judah, and took care of him for the rest of his life.

6. QUOTE IT: When the scribes and Pharisees brought a woman caught in adultery to Jesus, Jesus told them, "He that is without sin among you. . ."

7. FILL IN THE BLANK: David showed great kindness to the son of Jonathan named _____.

8. MULTIPLE CHOICE: Jesus was kind to the woman at the well who lived in
    a. Jericho
    b. Jerusalem
    c. Bethlehem
    d. Samaria

9. QUOTE IT: When the lame man asked Peter for money, Peter replied, "Silver and gold have I none, but such as I have I give thee. . . ."

10. MULTIPLE CHOICE: Ruth came to Boaz's attention because
    a. she gave money to the poor of Bethlehem
    b. she was gleaning in his field
    c. she was a servant in his house
    d. she was raising eleven children

Quiz 9
COURAGE, MAN, COURAGE!

It's a scary world out there. . .but God is bigger and stronger than anything that can come against us. He provides all the courage we need to win. So go ahead—boldly answer these questions on biblical courage!

1. QUOTE IT: The rulers and elders of Israel noted about Peter and John, after seeing their "boldness" in preaching salvation, that "they had. . ."

2. MULTIPLE CHOICE: Who received the following message from God: "Be strong and of a good courage: for unto this people shalt thou divide for an inheritance the land, which I sware unto their fathers to give them"?
  a. Moses
  b. David
  c. Joshua
  d. Saul

3. TRUE OR TRICK: Courage is listed as a "fruit of the Spirit" in Galatians 5:22–23.

4. QUOTE IT: How does the book of Hebrews tell Christians to approach "the throne of grace"?

5. MULTIPLE CHOICE: What formerly secret follower of Jesus "went in boldly unto Pilate" and asked to bury the Lord's body?

    a. Andrew
    b. John Mark
    c. Cleopas
    d. Joseph of Arimathea

6. QUOTE IT: What does the psalmist say God will do if you are "of good courage"?

7. MULTIPLE CHOICE: What rather uncourageous man gained boldness to fight the Midianites after God performed two miracles with fleece and dew?

    a. Gideon
    b. Aaron
    c. Isaac
    d. Eliab

8. TRUE OR TRICK: The apostle Paul wrote to Titus that "God hath not given us the spirit of fear."

9. QUOTE IT: What does the first letter of John say "casteth out fear"?

10. MULTIPLE CHOICE: What weapon—guided by God's power—did young David use to defeat the Philistine giant Goliath?

    a. spear
    b. sling
    c. bow and arrow
    d. club

Quiz 10
COWS AND OTHER LIVESTOCK

In biblical times, a man's wealth was often measured by how many animals he owned and his wealth was considered a blessing from God. How much do you know about biblical livestock?

1. MULTIPLE CHOICE: In the Psalms, God says He owns the cattle
   a. in all the earth
   b. in all Israel
   c. on a thousand hills
   d. in all the land

2. TRUE OR TRICK: Abraham and Lot separated because they both had so much livestock that the land couldn't support them both.

3. FILL IN THE BLANK: In the parable of the lost sheep, the shepherd left _____ sheep to go find the lost one.

4. MULTIPLE CHOICE: In Malachi's prophecy, God told the priests that by offering blind, lame, and sick animals for sacrifice, the priests had
   a. ruined the priesthood
   b. despised God's name
   c. become cursed
   d. all of the above

5. QUOTE IT: Isaiah 53:6 says, "All we like sheep have gone astray. . ."

6. FILL IN THE BLANK: When the prodigal son ran away from his father, he ended up tending to _____ in a foreign country.

7. TRUE OR TRICK: Laban paid Jacob with speckled and spotted cows and goats and brown sheep.

8. FILL IN THE BLANK: When God stayed Abraham's hand from sacrificing Isaac, Abraham discovered a _____ in the thicket to use for sacrifice.

9. TRUE OR TRICK: Two of the judges of Israel are described by how many colts they had.

10. MULTIPLE CHOICE: When God gave His commands for how the king should act, God specifically said that the king should not multiply horses in order to
   a. show his wealth
   b. return to Egypt
   c. go to war
   d. give them to his princes

Quiz 11
THE CRUCIFIXION

The most horrible day in all of history was the day Jesus was crucified. But He endured because of the joy He knew its aftermath would bring. How much do you know about what actually happened that day?

1. TRUE OR TRICK: Peter was the only disciple who watched the crucifixion.

2. MULTIPLE CHOICE: When Jesus stumbled, the man the Romans made carry Jesus' cross was
    a. Simon Peter
    b. Simon of Cyrene
    c. Simon the Zealot
    d. Simon the Sorcerer

3. FILL IN THE BLANK: The sign on Jesus' cross that read JESUS OF NAZARETH THE KING OF THE JEWS was written in _____ different languages.

4. QUOTE IT: When the chief priests tried to get Pilate to change the sign to read, "He said, I am King of the Jews," Pilate replied, "What I have written. . ."

5. QUOTE IT: The first thing Jesus said while He was on the cross was. . .

6. MULTIPLE CHOICE: The soldiers gambled for Jesus' coat because they

    a. wanted to keep it in one piece

    b. were bored

    c. had a right to it

    d. gambled on everything

7. QUOTE IT: Jesus told the thief who repented, "Today..."

8. TRUE OR TRICK: When Jesus died, the veil in the temple was torn in two from bottom to top.

9. FILL IN THE BLANK: Darkness covered all the earth for _____ hours.

10. TRUE OR TRICK: When Jesus died, graves opened and many people arose.

Quiz 12
DARING DANIEL

Perhaps the most famous story about Daniel is the one about the lions' den. But Daniel did many, many other things. What do you know about the rest of his life?

1. FILL IN THE BLANK: Daniel's Babylonian name was

_____.

2. TRUE OR TRICK: Daniel interpreted a dream for King Darius because the wise men couldn't.

3. MULTIPLE CHOICE: How many days did Daniel and his friends eat the food they requested as a test?
    a. three
    b. seven
    c. ten
    d. fourteen

4. FILL IN THE BLANK: Daniel knelt _____ times a day to pray.

5. TRUE OR TRICK: Before Daniel was taken captive to Babylon, he was a prince of Judah.

6. FILL IN THE BLANK: God gave Daniel _____ and skill in all learning and _____.

7. QUOTE IT: "Daniel purposed in his heart that he..."

8. TRUE OR TRICK: Daniel interpreted the handwriting on the wall for Nebuchadnezzar.

9. TRUE OR TRICK: Daniel was visited by the angel Michael.

10. MULTIPLE CHOICE: At the end of his visions, Daniel was told by God
    a. to go his way
    b. that the words were sealed until the end of time
    c. not to tell anyone
    d. a and b

Quiz 13
DAVID, THE MAN AFTER GOD'S OWN HEART

The account of David and Goliath is still one of the most popular stories told. But killing Goliath was only a small part of the whole of David's life. What do you know about the rest?

1. MULTIPLE CHOICE: Who, in one of his sermons, actually described David as a man after God's own heart?
    a. Jesus
    b. Stephen
    c. Paul
    d. Peter

2. TRUE OR TRICK: Ruth and Boaz were David's great-grandparents.

3. FILL IN THE BLANK: David was from the tribe of
_____.

4. QUOTE IT: When Samuel went to anoint David, God told Samuel, "Man looketh on the outward appearance..."

5. TRUE OR TRICK: David set up the system of worship in the temple.

6. MULTIPLE CHOICE: When David brought the ark of the covenant to Jerusalem, he danced before it and his wife, Michal,

    a. danced with him

    b. paid no attention

    c. despised him in her heart

    d. made a feast for him

7. FILL IN THE BLANK: David made _____ to praise the Lord.

8. QUOTE IT: After David sinned with Bathsheba, the prophet Nathan told the king a story. When David said that the man in the story should surely die, Nathan said…

9. TRUE OR TRICK: Hiding from King Saul, the hungry David and his men refused to eat showbread because it was only for the priests.

10. TRUE OR TRICK: At one time, David lived among the Philistines for more than a year.

Quiz 14
DAYS OF CREATION

God created everything in a specific order and He created it to be perfect. What do you know about His creation?

1. FILL IN THE BLANK: The first things God created were _____.

2. QUOTE IT: And God said, "Let there be light. . ."

3. TRUE OR TRICK: God named Day, Night, and Heaven.

4. FILL IN THE BLANK: The first things the earth brought forth were _____.

5. MULTIPLE CHOICE: On the fourth day God created
   a. fish
   b. animals
   c. the sun, moon, and stars
   d. man

6. FILL IN THE BLANK: God made the beast of the earth after his _____, and cattle after their _____.

7. MULTIPLE CHOICE: Which of the following was *not* marked by the lights in the firmament of heaven?

    a. signs
    b. seasons
    c. days
    d. months

8. TRUE OR TRICK: God called for sea creatures before He spoke birds into existence.

9. QUOTE IT: And God said, "Let us make man. . ."

10. FILL IN THE BLANK: The last thing God created was _____.

Quiz 15
DEVIL AND DEMONS

In Jesus' day, demon possession was common, but even now we fight spiritual battles against evil ones. To succeed, we need to understand the enemy. How prepared are you to fight?

1. QUOTE IT: "Thou believest that there is one God; thou doest well: the devils also believe. . ."

2. TRUE OR TRICK: The Pharisees said Jesus could only cast out devils because He worked for the prince of devils, Beelzebub.

3. QUOTE IT: When Jesus' disciples asked Him why they couldn't cast a demon out of a man's son, Jesus replied, "This kind goeth not out but by. . ."

4. MULTIPLE CHOICE: Mary Magdalene was cleansed from how many demons?
   a. three
   b. seven
   c. ten
   d. twenty-one

5. FILL IN THE BLANK: God gives us armor to stand against the wiles of the devil. This armor includes the helmet of _____, the breastplate of _____, and the shield of _____.

6. TRUE OR TRICK: Demons cannot recognize Jesus.

7. MULTIPLE CHOICE: People were healed from their diseases and demon possession when they were brought
    a. pieces of Jesus' robe
    b. water from the Jordan River
    c. Paul's handkerchiefs
    d. the bones of Moses

8. TRUE OR TRICK: Satan can present himself before God.

9. MULTIPLE CHOICE: Jesus said He saw Satan fall from heaven
    a. as a dove
    b. as lightning
    c. as a shooting star
    d. as a rock

10. QUOTE IT: Jesus responded to Satan's temptation by saying, "It is written again, Thou shalt not tempt. . ."

Quiz 16
DREAMS AND DREAMERS

All throughout the Bible God spoke to people in dreams. How many of these answers can you dream up?

1. MULTIPLE CHOICE: How many times did an angel appear to Joseph, the husband of Mary?

    a. once
    b. twice
    c. three times
    d. never

2. FILL IN THE BLANK: When Joseph was in jail in Egypt, he interpreted dreams for two of Pharaoh's servants: his _____ and _____.

3. TRUE OR TRICK: Pilate suffered all day because he had a nightmare that Jesus was a just man being convicted of a crime He did not commit.

4. QUOTE IT: When Jacob woke from his dream of a ladder reaching to heaven, he said, "Surely the LORD is in this place and. . ."

5. MULTIPLE CHOICE: Who was given a vision of unclean animals and told to eat them?

    a. James

    b. Peter

    c. Paul

    d. John

6. TRUE OR TRICK: God let Gideon overhear a Midianite tell a fellow soldier about his dream that indicated Gideon's army would prevail.

7. MULTIPLE CHOICE: When Peter, in his sermon on the day of Pentecost, mentioned old men dreaming dreams, which prophet was he referring to?

    a. Isaiah

    b. Jeremiah

    c. Joel

    d. Zechariah

8. QUOTE IT: God appeared to Solomon in a dream and told Solomon. . .

9. MULTIPLE CHOICE: Who did God refuse to answer in dreams, by Urim, or by prophets?

    a. King Saul

    b. Samson

    c. King Ahab

    d. one of the sons of the prophets

10. TRUE OR TRICK: Job told God that the dreams God sent him scared him.

Quiz 17

EARTHQUAKES AND OTHER DISASTERS

The word *earthquake* can strike fear in many hearts, as can the mention of any number of other disasters. What do you know about these biblical calamities?

1. MULTIPLE CHOICE: Which of the following did *not* experience an earthquake, at least in the biblical record?

    a. Elijah
    b. Paul and Silas
    c. Jesus
    d. Abraham

2. FILL IN THE BLANK: During the flood in Noah's time, it rained _____ days and _____ nights.

3. MULTIPLE CHOICE: The ground opened up and swallowed Korah and all he had because he rebelled against God and

    a. David
    b. Moses
    c. Samuel
    d. Othniel

4. TRUE OR TRICK: God once saved Israel by raining hailstones down on their enemy, the Midianites.

5. MULTIPLE CHOICE: The prophet who told King Ahab that God was going to send drought on Israel was
    a. Isaiah
    b. Jeremiah
    c. Elijah
    d. Elisha

6. FILL IN THE BLANK: Joseph told Pharaoh that the interpretation of his dreams about the cows and the corn meant the coming of a _____.

7. QUOTE IT: When a storm threatened to capsize the boat that Jesus and His disciples were in, Jesus calmed the storm by saying. . .

8. QUOTE IT: In the end times, people want the rocks and the mountains to fall on them to save them from. . .

9. TRUE OR TRICK: Naomi and her family moved from Bethlehem to Moab because there was a plague in Judah.

10. MULTIPLE CHOICE: Which of the following plagues on Egypt was duplicated by Pharaoh's magicians?
    a. boils on man and beast
    b. hail
    c. frogs
    d. death of the firstborn

Quiz 18
EMMANUEL

Matthew 1:23 says, "They shall call his name Emmanuel, which being interpreted is, God with us." What else do you know about Jesus, "God with us"?

1. QUOTE IT: Matthew 1:21 says, "Thou shalt call his name JESUS: for. . ."

2. FILL IN THE BLANK: Jesus is the Lamb of God and the _____ of the tribe of Judah.

3. MULTIPLE CHOICE: When the Pharisees demanded to know where Jesus' authority came from, He said He would answer their question if they answered His. The question Jesus asked was:
    a. By what authority do you do things?
    b. Who is my neighbor?
    c. The baptism of John, was it from heaven, or of men?
    d. Is it lawful for Herod to have his brother's wife?

4. TRUE OR TRICK: John the Baptist asked Jesus, "Art thou he that should come? or look we for another?"

5. MULTIPLE CHOICE: How old was Jesus when He began His public ministry?

    a. twelve

    b. twenty-two

    c. thirty

    d. forty-seven

6. TRUE OR TRICK: When Jesus asked His disciples, "Whom do men say that I am?" one of the answers was John the Baptist.

7. QUOTE IT: When Jesus asked His disciples, "Whom say ye that I am?" Peter replied, "Thou art..."

8. QUOTE IT: When the Pharisees tried to trap Jesus by asking Him if it was lawful to give tribute to Caesar, Jesus replied...

9. QUOTE IT: To prove that Jesus had the power to forgive sins, Jesus healed the man with the palsy and told him, "Arise, and..."

10. MULTIPLE CHOICE: When the Pharisees criticized Jesus' disciples for plucking and eating corn on the Sabbath, Jesus replied:

    a. "The Sabbath was made for man, not man for the Sabbath"

    b. with a story about David and his men eating the showbread

    c. "The Son of Man is Lord of the Sabbath"

    d. all of the above

Quiz 19
EXCELLENT ESTHER

The story of Esther's courage is one we all should know. What else do you know about Esther's life?

1. TRUE OR TRICK: The book of Esther never mentions the name of God.

2. MULTIPLE CHOICE: Esther's Hebrew name was
    a. Rebekah
    b. Dinah
    c. Hadassah
    d. Tamar

3. FILL IN THE BLANK: Mordecai's family relationship to Esther was _____.

4. FILL IN THE BLANK: Mordecai and Esther were from the tribe of _____.

5. MULTIPLE CHOICE: Haman plotted to kill all the Jews because he hated Mordecai—and he hated Mordecai because:
    a. he was Esther's guardian
    b. he was second only to the king
    c. he wouldn't bow or show reverence to Haman
    d. he spit on Haman

6. QUOTE IT: When the king asked Esther what she wanted, she replied, "Let the king and Haman come this day unto. . ."

7. TRUE OR TRICK: When the king asked Haman's advice for honoring someone, Haman thought it would be him. . .but the king meant Mordecai.

8. FILL IN THE BLANK: The queen that Esther replaced was named _____.

9. MULTIPLE CHOICE: The story of Esther takes place in
    a. Egypt
    b. Persia
    c. Israel
    d. Babylon

10. TRUE OR TRICK: Because the king could not revoke his decree to slaughter the Jews, he amended it to allow the Jews to defend themselves.

Quiz 20
FALSE GODS

The Israelites created a lot of problems for themselves by worshipping false gods. Here are just a few of the many that led them astray.

1. QUOTE IT: The first of the ten commandments says, "I am the LORD thy God. Thou shalt have. . ."

2. TRUE OR TRICK: When the Philistines stole the ark of the covenant and took it to the temple of their god, the statue of Dagon fell face down in front of the ark.

3. MULTIPLE CHOICE: The goddess Diana is the only mention of an idol in the New Testament. Her shrine was in
   a. Corinth
   b. Colosse
   c. Laodicea
   d. Ephesus

4. MULTIPLE CHOICE: Hezekiah destroyed Nehushtan, which was another name for
   a. the brass snake Moses made in the wilderness
   b. the golden calf Aaron made
   c. the ephod Gideon made
   d. Baal

5. FILL IN THE BLANK: The wicked queen directly responsible for bringing Baal worship to Israel was _____.

6. TRUE OR TRICK: The Greek sea god Poseidon is mentioned in the Bible.

7. MULTIPLE CHOICE: What king of Israel was the first to build places for the worship of Chemosh and Molech?
    a. Ahab
    b. Jehu
    c. Solomon
    d. Zimri

8. TRUE OR TRICK: Someone besides Aaron also made golden calves for Israel to worship.

9. MULTIPLE CHOICE: What did the godly King Josiah change places of idolatry into?
    a. meadows
    b. potters' fields
    c. wastelands
    d. cemeteries

10. FILL IN THE BLANK: The church in Corinth was divided over _____ offered to idols.

Quiz 21
FEAR NOT!

The psalmist said that the Lord had delivered him from all fear (Psalm 34:4). Can these biblical admonitions and examples help calm your fears?

1. FILL IN THE BLANK: "Perfect _____ casteth out fear."

2. MULTIPLE CHOICE: To whom was God speaking when He said, "Have not I commanded thee? Be strong and of a good courage; be not afraid"?
    a. Moses
    b. Abraham
    c. Joshua
    d. Gideon

3. QUOTE IT: 2 Timothy 1:7 says that God has not given us "the spirit of fear; but of power, and of love, and. . ."

4. TRUE OR TRICK: Jesus said we should fear those who can kill the body.

5. MULTIPLE CHOICE: When the angel at Jesus' tomb said, "Fear not," he was talking to
  a. Peter and John
  b. the Roman soldiers
  c. Joseph of Arimathea
  d. Mary Magdalene and another Mary

6. TRUE OR TRICK: After an angel told Hagar, "Fear not," she took Ishmael back to Abraham.

7. QUOTE IT: The prophet Isaiah quoted God as saying, "I will uphold thee with. . ."

8. MULTIPLE CHOICE: When his brothers bowed before him, Joseph said, "Fear not: for. . ."
  a. "I won't harm you"
  b. "I am your brother"
  c. "I love you"
  d. "am I in the place of God?"

9. FILL IN THE BLANK: The Lord told Abraham not to fear because He was Abraham's shield and exceeding great _____.

10. QUOTE IT: When Jesus walked on the water to His disciples' boat, He told them not to be afraid because. . .

Quiz 22
FIRE!

Fire can be good or dangerous. A warm fire on a cold day can be comforting, but fire out of control can be destructive. What do you know about biblical fires?

1. QUOTE IT: When Shadrach, Meshach, and Abednego were in the fiery furnace, Nebuchadnezzar said he saw four men walking around inside—and the form of the fourth man was "like the. . ."

2. QUOTE IT: Jesus said the everlasting fire was prepared for. . .

3. MULTIPLE CHOICE: Which prophet of God sat on a mountain and called down fire from heaven to consume the king's soldiers who had come to arrest him?
   a. Ezekiel
   b. Daniel
   c. Elijah
   d. Isaiah

4. TRUE OR TRICK: One of the plagues on Egypt was fire.

5. FILL IN THE BLANK: God destroyed Sodom and Gomorrah with fire and _____.

6. FILL IN THE BLANK: The judge of Israel who used foxes and firebrands to burn the Philistine's cornfields was _____.

7. TRUE OR TRICK: John the Baptist said that he baptized with water but the One coming after him would baptize with the Holy Spirit and fire.

8. FILL IN THE BLANK: Tongues of fire appeared above the heads of the disciples on the day of _____.

9. MULTIPLE CHOICE: To whom was the prophet Amos referring when he said, "You were as a firebrand plucked out of the burning"?
  a. himself
  b. King Hezekiah
  c. Jeremiah
  d. Israel

10. QUOTE IT: Jesus said hell is where the fire is not quenched and. . .

Quiz 23
FOUR-SYLLABLE NAMES

What's in a name? Sometimes four syllables. Do you know these?

1. MULTIPLE CHOICE: Eleazar was the son of
    a. Moses
    b. Aaron
    c. Seth
    d. Lot

2. FILL IN THE BLANK: A testimony to Hezekiah's faithfulness is given in the prophetic book of _____.

3. QUOTE IT: When the pregnant Mary went to see her expectant relative Elizabeth, the latter greeted her by saying, "Blessed art thou among women, and. . ."

4. MULTIPLE CHOICE: Elimelech was
    a. Naomi's husband
    b. high priest during David's reign
    c. one of the sons of the prophets
    d. Abraham's servant

5. FILL IN THE BLANK: Onesimus is the subject of the book of _____.

6. QUOTE IT: "And all the days of Methuselah were. . ."

7. TRUE OR TRICK: Bartimaeus was a blind man healed by Jesus.

8. TRUE OR TRICK: Melchizedek was king of Salem.

9. MULTIPLE CHOICE: Solomon's son who followed him as king was
    a. Rehoboam
    b. Jeroboam
    c. Hezekiah
    d. Ahaziah

10. TRUE OR TRICK: Nicodemus was the name of a beggar carried to the bosom of Abraham by angels.

Quiz 24
GENEALOGIES

Many people skip over the lists of "begats" in the Bible. But you can learn a lot about people from their family connections. What do you know about these biblical parents and children?

1. FILL IN THE BLANK: After Cain killed Abel, Adam and Eve had another son whom they named _____.

2. TRUE OR TRICK: Isaac's favorite son was Jacob and Rebekah's favorite was Esau.

3. FILL IN THE BLANK: Noah's three sons were named _____, _____, and _____.

4. TRUE OR TRICK: When a messenger brought the news that his sons, Hophni and Phinehas, had been slain in battle, ninety-eight-year-old Eli fell backward off his seat, broke his neck, and died.

5. FILL IN THE BLANK: Laban's two daughters were _____ and _____.

6. MULTIPLE CHOICE: The daughter of Jacob mentioned in scripture is:

    a. Tamar

    b. Abigail

    c. Dinah

    d. Hagar

7. MULTIPLE CHOICE: The only judge of Israel who appointed himself (rather than being appointed by God) was Abimelech, the son of

    a. Jephthah

    b. Othniel

    c. Deborah

    d. Gideon

8. MULTIPLE CHOICE: How many sons did Moses have?

    a. two

    b. five

    c. seven

    d. twelve

9. FILL IN THE BLANK: The two sons that Rachel gave birth to were _____ and _____.

10. TRUE OR TRICK: One of David's sons killed another of the king's sons.

Quiz 25
GETTING FROM HERE TO THERE

In this day of speedy cars and jets, we take traveling for granted. But things were much slower and more difficult in biblical times. Could you have traveled as these people did?

1. QUOTE IT: "How beautiful upon the mountains are the feet of him. . ."

2. MULTIPLE CHOICE: Who sang "the horse and his rider hath he thrown into the sea"?
    a. Moses
    b. all the children of Israel
    c. Miriam
    d. all of the above

3. MULTIPLE CHOICE: When his donkey spoke to him, Balaam was traveling
    a. to see King Balak
    b. to curse the people of Israel
    c. with the princes of Moab
    d. all of the above

4. FILL IN THE BLANK: In the days of the judges, Canaanite chariots were made of _____.

5. TRUE OR TRICK: Jehu was famous for driving his chariot furiously.

6. MULTIPLE CHOICE: What miracle had Jesus just performed before He walked on the water to His disciples' boat?
- a. healing a lame man
- b. giving a blind man his sight
- c. feeding the five thousand
- d. raising Lazarus from the dead

7. TRUE OR TRICK: The children of Israel were told to walk around Jericho once a day for seven days.

8. TRUE OR TRICK: After Elijah defeated the prophets of Baal, the prophet outran the chariot of King Ahab to the city of Jezreel.

9. MULTIPLE CHOICE: When David took food from his father to his brothers in King Saul's camp, David
- a. rode a horse
- b. rode a camel
- c. drove a chariot
- d. ran to the valley of Elah

10. TRUE OR TRICK: When the Babylonians took Judah's King Jehoiakim in fetters to Babylon, they made the prisoner walk the whole way behind Nebuchadnezzar's chariot.

Quiz 26
GIFTED

Gifted people often make the news. What do you know about the biblical gifts and abilities that God gave to His followers?

1. TRUE OR TRICK: When Samson's hair was cut, the Lord departed from him.

2. FILL IN THE BLANK: In addition to being a mighty valiant man, David was skilled in playing the _____.

3. FILL IN THE BLANK: "There are diversities of gifts, but the same _____. And there are differences of administrations, but the same _____. And there are diversities of operations, but it is the same _____ which worketh all in all."

4. MULTIPLE CHOICE: Who tried to avoid God's calling by complaining he was a poor speaker?
    a. Moses
    b. David
    c. Joshua
    d. Zephaniah

5. QUOTE IT: Elisha asked of his mentor Elijah, "I pray thee, let. . ."

6. MULTIPLE CHOICE: Who received the gift of God through the laying on of Paul's hands?
a. Gaius
b. Timothy
c. Luke
d. Titus

7. TRUE OR TRICK: When the Spirit of the Lord was on him, King Saul could prophesy.

8. FILL IN THE BLANK: God gave Paul the gift of being a minister and a witness to _____.

9. FILL IN THE BLANK: The prophet who refused God's gift of prophecy and tried to run away from God was _____.

10. TRUE OR TRICK: God gifts people to be pastors and evangelists.

Quiz 27
THE GOLDEN RULE

Most people seem to have heard of the Golden Rule—even people who don't follow Jesus. But you know Jesus is the author of the Golden Rule. What else do you know about it?

1. MULTIPLE CHOICE: Where in the Bible do you find the Golden Rule?
    a. Matthew
    b. Luke
    c. John
    d. a and b

2. TRUE OR TRICK: The Golden Rule is included in Jesus' Sermon on the Mount.

3. QUOTE IT: "All things whatsoever ye would that men should do to you. . ."

4. MULTIPLE CHOICE: Which parable did Jesus tell that exemplified the Golden Rule?
    a. the sower and the seed
    b. the Pharisee and the publican
    c. the Good Samaritan
    d. the rich fool

5. TRUE OR TRICK: When the rich young ruler asked Jesus what he could do to inherit eternal life, Jesus told him to follow the Golden Rule.

6. MULTIPLE CHOICE: When Jesus spoke the Golden Rule, He was talking to
    a. his twelve disciples
    b. Mary, Martha, and Lazarus
    c. multitudes
    d. the scribes and Pharisees

7. MULTIPLE CHOICE: Immediately before talking about the Golden Rule, Jesus was talking about
    a. God giving good things to those who ask Him
    b. God's kingdom
    c. the narrow and wide gates
    d. building your house on a rock, not sand

8. QUOTE IT: "Give to every man that. . ."

9. FILL IN THE BLANKS: Jesus said the Golden Rule summarized the _____ and the _____.

10. TRUE OR TRICK: Jesus called His teaching "the Golden Rule."

Quiz 28
HEAVEN ABOVE

Most people have their own ideas about what heaven is and what it is like. What do you know of how the Bible describes heaven?

1. FILL IN THE BLANK: The only tree mentioned as being on earth and in heaven is the tree of _____.

2. QUOTE IT: The Sadducees, who didn't even believe in resurrection, tried to trick Jesus with a complicated question about marriage in the afterlife. Jesus replied they didn't know the scripture that says no one will marry then but will be. . .

3. FILL IN THE BLANK: "Lay up for yourselves _____ in heaven."

4. TRUE OR TRICK: The apostle Paul said that he had been caught up to the third heaven.

5. FILL IN THE BLANK: When the seventh seal of Revelation was opened, there was _____ in heaven.

6. QUOTE IT: John said he saw a new heaven and a new earth, for the first heaven and the first earth. . .

7. FILL IN THE BLANKS: In heaven, Jesus sits at the
_____ _____ of the throne of God.

8. TRUE OR TRICK: There is a rainbow around God's throne in heaven.

9. TRUE OR TRICK: As Stephen was being stoned, he saw the heavens opened and God the Father standing to receive him.

10. MULTIPLE CHOICE: Around God's throne in heaven there are _____ seats.

    a. two
    b. seven
    c. twelve
    d. twenty-four

Quiz 29
HI, PRIESTS

Jesus is our Great High Priest and the ultimate example of what a priest should be. What do you know about these other biblical priests?

1. FILL IN THE BLANK: The first high priest mentioned in the Bible was _____.

2. TRUE OR TRICK: A person who fled to a city of refuge had to stay there until the current high priest died.

3. TRUE OR TRICK: The only recorded instance of there being two high priests at the same time was in Jesus' day.

4. QUOTE IT: On the high priest's headdress was a gold plate engraved with. . .

5. FILL IN THE BLANK: _____ appointed Aaron and his sons as the first priests of Israel.

6. FILL IN THE BLANK: In days of the early church, the high priests belonged to the sect of the _____.

7. MULTIPLE CHOICE: All priests were from the tribe of
    a. Judah
    b. Benjamin
    c. Levi
    d. Dan

8. MULTIPLE CHOICE: In the book of Malachi, God calls the priests to account because they
    a. worshipped idols
    b. despised His name
    c. stole from the temple treasury
    d. all of the above

9. TRUE OR TRICK: John the Baptist's father, Zacharias, was a priest.

10. TRUE OR TRICK: The apostle Paul once had to apologize for insulting the high priest.

Quiz 30
HOLY, HOLY, HOLY

Throughout the Bible, God shows us different attributes of Himself. How well do you know Him and His characteristics?

1. QUOTE IT: When Hagar ran away from Sarah and was lost in the wilderness, the Lord came to speak to her. Hagar called Him. . .

2. MULTIPLE CHOICE: At the beginning of the Ten Commandments, God describes Himself as the Lord God who
    a. created the heavens and the earth
    b. chose Israel to be His people
    c. brought Israel out of the land of Egypt
    d. loved His people before the foundation of the earth

3. FILL IN THE BLANK: When Abraham found a ram in a thicket to sacrifice instead of his son Isaac, he called the name of the place _____.

4. TRUE OR TRICK: James calls God's Word the perfect law of grace.

5. MULTIPLE CHOICE: Which of the following is *not* a name of God used in Psalms?
- a. Shepherd
- b. Strong Rock
- c. Mighty God of Abraham
- d. Saving Strength of His Anointed

6. QUOTE IT: "Behold, what manner of love the Father hath bestowed upon us, that we should be called. . ."

7. MULTIPLE CHOICE: We know that God works all things out for our good for those of us who love Him and
- a. obey Him
- b. worship Him
- c. are called according to His purpose
- d. follow Him

8. FILL IN THE BLANKS: Psalm 100:5 says that the Lord is _____; His mercy is _____; and His truth _____ to all generations.

9. TRUE OR TRICK: Psalm 139 says God knows us from the moment of birth.

10. FILL IN THE BLANKS: The Lord will judge the world in _____ and minister judgment to the people in _____.

Quiz 31
THE HUMAN BODY

God said He knew Jeremiah before he was formed in his mother's belly (Jeremiah 1:5). Our bodies are designed by God to enable us to do His work. Do you know what the Bible says about the human frame?

1. QUOTE IT: The psalmist says people are "fearfully and..."

2. FILL IN THE BLANKS: "For _____ thou art, and unto _____ shalt thou return."

3. TRUE OR TRICK: King Saul stood head and shoulders above the crowd.

4. TRUE OR TRICK: When the Israelites were fighting the Amalekites, they only prevailed as long as Moses held up his hand over the battlefield.

5. MULTIPLE CHOICE: When Delilah sought the source of Samson's strength, he lied—saying he would lose his strength if he was bound with how many fresh bowstrings?
    a. three
    b. five
    c. seven
    d. ten

6. FILL IN THE BLANK: The prophet Isaiah wrote, "Behold, the Lord's _____ is not shortened, that it cannot save."

7. QUOTE IT: "Out of the same mouth proceedeth. . ."

8. TRUE OR TRICK: James said that the hardest part of the body to tame is the eye.

9. MULTIPLE CHOICE: The Proverbs say that a little sleep, a little folding of the hands to rest is the way to
    a. wealth
    b. health
    c. poverty
    d. hunger

10. FILL IN THE BLANK: God had the prophet _____ prophesy to a valley of dry bones that were joined together and reanimated.

Quiz 32
HUSBANDS AND WIVES

In the Bible, some husbands married good wives and some wives married good husbands. And then there were some not-so-good husbands and wives, just like today.

1. QUOTE IT: When Queen Vashti disobeyed her husband, King Ahasuerus, he issued a decree to every person under his rule that said "every man should. . ."

2. TRUE OR TRICK: Solomon had three hundred wives and seven hundred concubines.

3. MULTIPLE CHOICE: Whose wives were a grief of mind to his parents?
   a. Judah
   b. Esau
   c. David
   d. Cain

4. QUOTE IT: When Joseph found out that Mary was with child, he "was minded to. . ."

5. MULTIPLE CHOICE: Which of the following wives was *not* found by a well?

    a. Rebekah

    b. Rachel

    c. Zipporah

    d. Bathsheba

6. FILL IN THE BLANK: The tentmakers who let Paul live with them were Priscilla and her husband _____.

7. TRUE OR TRICK: David was married to one of King Saul's daughters.

8. QUOTE IT: When confronted with his sin, Adam cast blame, saying, "the woman whom thou gavest to be with me..."

9. TRUE OR TRICK: Samson's first wife refused to leave her father's house.

10. FILL IN THE BLANKS: The Proverbs say, "Whoso findeth a wife findeth a _____ _____."

Quiz 33
I AM

In Exodus, God called Himself "I AM." In the Gospels, Jesus finished that sentence with various descriptions of Himself. How much do you know about their statements?

1. FILL IN THE BLANK: When God said, "Thus shalt thou say unto the children of Israel, I AM hath sent me unto you," He was speaking to _____.

2. QUOTE IT: Jesus told Thomas, "I am the way, the truth, and the life. . ."

3. FILL IN THE BLANK: God said His people were not to worship other gods because "I the LORD thy God am a _____ God."

4. QUOTE IT: In the Old Testament, manna was the bread from heaven. In the New Testament, Jesus said, "I am. . ."

5. MULTIPLE CHOICE: What event immediately preceded Jesus saying, "I am the light of the world"?
   a. the feeding of the five thousand
   b. the raising of Lazarus
   c. the forgiving of a woman caught in adultery
   d. the cursing of the barren fig tree

6. MULTIPLE CHOICE: On how many occasions did God speak from heaven and say "I am well pleased" in His beloved Son, Jesus?

    a. one
    b. two
    c. three
    d. four

7. QUOTE IT: When Saul was blinded by the light on his way to Damascus, he said, "Who art thou, Lord?" And Jesus replied, "I am. . ."

8. FILL IN THE BLANKS: God told Moses, "I am the God of thy father" and these three people: _____, _____, and _____.

9. MULTIPLE CHOICE: In the book of Revelation, Jesus introduced Himself to John by saying, "I am. . ."

    a. the Alpha and Omega
    b. the first and last
    c. the source and completion
    d. a and b

10. FILL IN THE BLANK: When Jesus said "I am the good shepherd," He also said, "I am the _____ of the sheep."

Quiz 34
IMPRISONED!

Many of God's people were persecuted and imprisoned, but they remained faithful to God. How well do you know these brave folks?

1. MULTIPLE CHOICE: From what land were the traders who bought Joseph from his brothers?

    a. Egypt
    b. Canaan
    c. the Orient
    d. Midian

2. QUOTE IT: When Paul and Silas were beaten and imprisoned in Philippi, at midnight they "prayed, and. . ."

3. TRUE OR TRICK: The prophet Jeremiah was put in a dungeon where he sank in the mud.

4. MULTIPLE CHOICE: King Herod put John the Baptist in prison because

    a. John said Herod wasn't really a king
    b. John rebuked Herod for stealing his brother's wife
    c. Herod didn't want John preaching about Jesus
    d. Herod wanted to please Pilate

5. TRUE OR TRICK: When Samson was in prison, the Philistines made him push a grinding wheel.

6. MULTIPLE CHOICE: What prophet did King Ahab imprison because he didn't like the man's message?
 a. Elijah
 b. Elisha
 c. Micaiah
 d. Isaiah

7. FILL IN THE BLANK: When John wrote the book of Revelation, he was exiled on the Isle of _____.

8. MULTIPLE CHOICE: Who broke the apostle Peter out of prison after he was arrested by King Herod?
 a. the other apostles
 b. Jesus
 c. the angel of the Lord
 d. Mary Magdalene

9. TRUE OR TRICK: The apostle Paul called himself "a prisoner of Jesus Christ."

10. QUOTE IT: In a parable of Jesus, "the King" commends people for visiting Him in prison. When they respond by asking when they saw Him in prison, He answers, "As ye have done it unto one of the least of these my brethren. . ."

Quiz 35
IN THE (BIBLE) KITCHEN

One of the most interesting foods in the Bible is *manna*, a word that means "what is it?" But there are plenty of other foods in scripture. What do you know about them?

1. TRUE OR TRICK: Manna continued to fall even after the children of Israel crossed the Jordan River into the promised land.

2. FILL IN THE BLANK: When Jesus was preparing to feed the five thousand, Philip told Jesus they didn't have enough money to buy bread for all those people. Then _____ brought to Jesus a small boy with five loaves and two fish.

3. TRUE OR TRICK: At the Last Supper, Jesus gave a sop (or piece of bread for dipping) to Peter.

4. QUOTE IT: When the prodigal son returned to his father, the older man honored the younger by preparing the fatted calf, saying, "Let us. . ."

5. MULTIPLE CHOICE: In the wilderness, when the children of Israel longed for the foods of their captivity in Egypt, which of the following was *not* one of those foods?
  a. cucumbers
  b. melons
  c. fish
  d. quail

6. TRUE OR TRICK: When a famine covered all of Canaan, Joseph's brothers went to Egypt to buy meat.

7. QUOTE IT: The Proverbs say, "Better is a dinner of herbs where love is, than a stalled ox. . ."

8. TRUE OR TRICK: Elisha once neutralized a poisoned stew by adding salt.

9. MULTIPLE CHOICE: Eli's sons took their priest's portion of the sacrifice to eat before the sacrifice was offered. God called them the sons of
  a. Belial
  b. Beelzebub
  c. betrayal
  d. bewilderment

10. QUOTE IT: Esau sold his birthright to Jacob for bread and lentil stew and thus "despised. . ."

Quiz 36
ISRAEL AND ISRAELITES

Jacob, whose name means "supplanter," had his name changed by God to Israel, which means "one who struggles with God." Then this name became the name of the whole nation. How much do you know about God's chosen people?

1. MULTIPLE CHOICE: God ordered one of his prophets to marry an unfaithful wife to illustrate how Israel treated Him. That prophet was

    a. Ezekiel

    b. Nahum

    c. Micah

    d. Hosea

2. TRUE OR TRICK: In the book of Malachi, when God told the Israelites, "I have loved you," they praised and thanked Him.

3. TRUE OR TRICK: The Israelites were only in the wilderness for a week when they started to complain.

4. MULTIPLE CHOICE: The twelve sons of Jacob became leaders of the twelve tribes of Israel. Jacob had his sons by _____ different women.

    a. two

    b. three

    c. four

    d. six

5. TRUE OR TRICK: There were six kings of Israel before the kingdom split into Israel and Judah.

6. QUOTE IT: God said to Israel, "Fear not: for I have redeemed thee, I have called thee by thy name. . ."

7. MULTIPLE CHOICE: The Israelites ended up as slaves in Egypt because Jacob originally moved his family there to escape

    a. fire

    b. marauders

    c. floods

    d. famine

8. TRUE OR TRICK: When the Israelites crossed the Red Sea, they crossed on dry land.

9. FILL IN THE BLANK: The tribe of Joseph was divided into the "half tribes" of _____ and _____.

10. MULTIPLE CHOICE: The apostle Paul's genealogy was through the tribe of

    a. Benjamin

    b. Judah

    c. Issachar

    d. Dan

Quiz 37
JEWELS AND JEWELRY

Many people enjoy a bright, sparkling piece of jewelry. Apparently Bible people did too. What do you know about the jewels of scripture?

1. FILL IN THE BLANK: The New Jerusalem has _____ gates, each one made of a single pearl.

2. MULTIPLE CHOICE: On the shoulders of the high priest's ephod were two stones engraved with the names of the children of Israel. Those stones were
    a. diamonds
    b. sapphires
    c. onyx
    d. rubies

3. TRUE OR TRICK: Aaron used gold necklaces donated by the people to make the golden calf.

4. QUOTE IT: Jesus told a parable of a merchant who discovered "one pearl. . ."

5. FILL IN THE BLANK: The price of a virtuous woman is far above _____.

6. MULTIPLE CHOICE: When Abraham's servant found Rebekah as a wife for Isaac, he immediately gave her
   a. a necklace of gold
   b. two necklaces of beaten silver
   c. a gold earring and two gold bracelets
   d. a gold crown

7. TRUE OR TRICK: When the Israelites defeated the Midianites, the captains of the host kept all the chains, bracelets, and earrings for themselves and gave all the livestock to the Lord as a sacrifice.

8. MULTIPLE CHOICE: Which of the following is *not* one of the precious stones used in the foundation of the New Jerusalem?
   a. sapphire
   b. emerald
   c. amethyst
   d. diamond

9. FILL IN THE BLANK: The Proverbs say that the lips of _____ are a precious jewel.

10. MULTIPLE CHOICE: Which New Testament writer warned Christians against being impressed by a church visitor's "goodly apparel" and gold ring?
   a. Matthew
   b. Paul
   c. Peter
   d. James

Quiz 38
JOB'S SAD STORY

"The patience of Job" is a common phrase. But how much do you know of what Job went through to acquire his famed patience?

1. MULTIPLE CHOICE: At the beginning of Job's testing, he had _____ children.

    a. two
    b. five
    c. seven
    d. ten

2. QUOTE IT: The Lord said to Satan, "Have you considered my servant, Job?" And Satan replied. . .

3. TRUE OR TRICK: Messengers who came to tell Job that his oxen, servants, sheep, camels, and children were all destroyed or stolen were interrupted by the arrival of the next messenger with bad news.

4. FILL IN THE BLANK: When Job's friends arrived they didn't speak for _____ days and nights.

5. MULTIPLE CHOICE: Which one of the following was *not* one of Job's friends?

    a. Eliphaz

    b. Bildad

    c. Zophar

    d. Zilpah

6. TRUE OR TRICK: The three friends finally stopped accusing Job because he was righteous in his own eyes.

7. QUOTE IT: When God answered Job, He said, "Where wast thou. . ."

8. MULTIPLE CHOICE: The Lord told Job's visitors that He was

    a. pleased with them

    b. willing to prosper them

    c. disappointed at the way they treated Job

    d. angry because of their unfaithfulness to Him

9. TRUE OR TRICK: After God vindicated Job, Job had five more children.

10. QUOTE IT: "So the LORD blessed the latter end of Job. . ."

Quiz 39
JOSHUA FIT THE BATTLE OF JERICHO

The one thing most people seem to know about the battle of Jericho is that "the walls came a-tumblin' down." What do you know about the rest of the battle?

1. TRUE OR TRICK: When the priests carried the ark of the covenant into the Jordan River near Jericho, the water stopped flowing and the people crossed.

2. QUOTE IT: When Joshua saw a man with his sword drawn, he asked the man, "Art thou for us, or for our adversaries?" The man replied, "Nay; but as . . ."

3. TRUE OR TRICK: In the lineup to march around Jericho, the priests carrying the ark went first.

4. MULTIPLE CHOICE: When the children of Israel were not marching around Jericho, they were camped at
    a. Kadesh-Barnea
    b. Jerusalem
    c. Gilgal
    d. Shiloh

5. QUOTE IT: "Now Jericho was straitly shut up because of the children of Israel. . ."

6. TRUE OR TRICK: The children of Israel marched around Jericho for six days so they would not violate the Sabbath.

7. FILL IN THE BLANK: Before the children of Israel could do battle with Jericho, God told Joshua to prepare them by _____ all the males who had not been previously.

8. TRUE OR TRICK: The only person living in Jericho that survived the fall of the city was Rahab.

9. QUOTE IT: "When they make a long blast with the ram's horn, and when ye hear the sound of the trumpet, all the people shall. . ."

10. MULTIPLE CHOICE: The person who stole some of the spoils from Jericho and put all of Israel at risk was
    a. Joshua
    b. Caleb
    c. Rahab
    d. Achan

Quiz 40
KINGS AND QUEENS

The Bible is full of kings and queens. Some were inspiring and some were awful. Here are some of each.

1. TRUE OR TRICK: David was the first king of Israel.

2. TRUE OR TRICK: Queen Vashti was married to the king of Persia.

3. MULTIPLE CHOICE: Eglon, king of Moab during the time of Israel's judges, was known for being
    a. tall
    b. handsome
    c. fat
    d. crippled

4. FILL IN THE BLANK: The evil queen Jezebel's death was foretold by the prophet _____.

5. MULTIPLE CHOICE: The queen of what nation visited Solomon to see his wisdom for herself?
    a. Sheba
    b. Salem
    c. Midian
    d. Egypt

6. QUOTE IT: According to Luke, besides being king of Judea, Herod was also called. . .

7. MULTIPLE CHOICE: When King Jeroboam tried to harm a prophet, he
   a. was struck blind
   b. was struck dead
   c. had his hand withered
   d. went bald

8. TRUE OR TRICK: Joash, the youngest king of Judah, was eight years old when he became king.

9. FILL IN THE BLANK: The Ethiopian eunuch in Acts 8 served queen _____.

10. QUOTE IT: The prophet Daniel wrote that God "changeth the times and the seasons. . ."

Quiz 41
KNIVES AND OTHER WEAPONS

It's true: the Bible can be a violent book. What do you know about the various weapons of Bible times?

1. MULTIPLE CHOICE: Ishmael's weapon of choice was a
  a. spear
  b. sword
  c. bow and arrow
  d. none—he didn't carry a weapon

2. FILL IN THE BLANK: Best friends _____ and _____ used arrows to signal messages between them.

3. MULTIPLE CHOICE: The special soldiers of the tribe of Benjamin who used slings were famous because
  a. there were seven hundred of them
  b. they could throw stones at a hair and not miss
  c. they were all left-handed
  d. all of the above

4. TRUE OR TRICK: A woman drove a tent stake through a man's head to save Israel from the Philistines.

5. MULTIPLE CHOICE: The judge of Israel that used the jawbone of a donkey to kill a thousand Philistines was

    a. Gideon

    b. Jephthah

    c. Othniel

    d. Samson

6. TRUE OR TRICK: Phinehas stopped a plague on the children of Israel by thrusting a javelin through a man and a woman.

7. FILL IN THE BLANKS: God gave Gideon's army of three hundred the unique weapons of _____ and _____ _____ _____ _____ to defeat the army of thousands of Midianites.

8. MULTIPLE CHOICE: How many stones did David take out of the brook when he went to fight Goliath?

    a. three

    b. four

    c. five

    d. a dozen

9. MULTIPLE CHOICE: The sword David used to cut off Goliath's head belonged to

    a. King Saul

    b. David's oldest brother

    c. the captain of Saul's army

    d. Goliath

10. QUOTE IT: When we are arming ourselves with the armor of God, we are to take "the sword of the Spirit, which is. . ."

Quiz 42
"KNOW" THIS

Someone has said the three hardest words to say are "I don't know." How in-the-know are you about these *knows* in the Bible?

1. QUOTE IT: In the book of John, Jesus said, "Ye shall know the truth, and. . ."

2. QUOTE IT: In Psalm 46:10, the Lord says, "Be still, and know. . ."

3. MULTIPLE CHOICE: The Proverbs say that their purpose is so that we can know

    a. wisdom and instruction

    b. the pleasure of good conduct

    c. the mind of God

    d. all of the above

4. TRUE OR TRICK: The Lord told Jeremiah that He knew the prophet when he was in the womb.

5. QUOTE IT: When God asked Cain where Abel was, Cain replied, "I know not. . ."

6. FILL IN THE BLANK: The Israelites' troubles in Egypt began when there arose a new Pharaoh who "knew not _____."

7. MULTIPLE CHOICE: On the cross, Jesus said, "Father, forgive them; for they know not..."
    a. You
    b. Me
    c. what they do
    d. that Satan is using them

8. TRUE OR TRICK: We are to take no thought for what we shall eat, drink, or wear because God knows we have need of all these things.

9. MULTIPLE CHOICE: We shall know the false prophets who come to us as wolves in sheep's clothing by their
    a. fruits
    b. words
    c. actions
    d. blasphemies

10. QUOTE IT: "By this shall all men know that ye are my disciples..."

Quiz 43
LANGUAGE ARTS

There are so many languages in the world today that it's impossible to know them all. But what do you know about these biblical languages?

1. MULTIPLE CHOICE: God confounded the languages at Babel because
    a. He had told the people to scatter throughout the world and they didn't
    b. nothing else could restrain them from what they imagined to do
    c. He was tired of their disobedience
    d. a and b

2. FILL IN THE BLANKS: In the Psalms, when the writer says, "There is no speech nor language, where their voice is not heard," he is referring to the _____ and the _____.

3. MULTIPLE CHOICE: When the king of Assyria sent his army captain to taunt the Israelites in Jerusalem, local officials begged the captain to speak in the _____ language which they understood, while most of their fellow Israelites did not.
    a. Persian
    b. Babylonian
    c. Syrian
    d. Egyptian

4. TRUE OR TRICK: When Nehemiah returned to help rebuild Jerusalem, he found that the Jews who still lived there had intermarried with non-Israelites and their children could not speak the Jews' language.

5. TRUE OR TRICK: Out of the 127 provinces under the rule of King Ahasuerus, only the Jews spoke a language different from the rest of the people.

6. QUOTE IT: Pilate put a sign on Jesus' cross written in Hebrew, Latin, and Greek. "And the writing was. . ."

7. TRUE OR TRICK: During a Jewish civil war, anyone who couldn't pronounce the word *Shibboleth* correctly was slain.

8. FILL IN THE BLANK: God told Ezekiel that He was not sending the prophet to "a people of a strange speech and of an hard language, but to the house of _____."

9. MULTIPLE CHOICE: In Daniel's day, King _____ sent a decree to all the people, nations, and languages of the world that Daniel's God had a kingdom that would never be destroyed.
    a. Nebuchadnezzar
    b. Cyrus
    c. Darius
    d. Belteshazzar

10. FILL IN THE BLANK: When Peter delivered his sermon on Pentecost and God translated it into the different languages of all the people there, mockers in the crowd said that Peter was _____.

Quiz 44
LEADERSHIP 101

There are plenty of leaders mentioned in the Bible in various roles. What do you know about these?

1. MULTIPLE CHOICE: After Joshua died, God sent _____ to be the first judge of Israel.
    a. Othniel
    b. Caleb
    c. Ehud
    d. Eleazar

2. TRUE OR TRICK: Ezra the priest led a caravan of Babylonian exiles back to the promised land.

3. FILL IN THE BLANK: Before he returned to help rebuild Jerusalem, Nehemiah was _____ to the king of Persia.

4. QUOTE IT: Joshua urged the Israelites to choose whom they would serve, saying, "As for me and my house. . ."

5. MULTIPLE CHOICE: Which of Jacob's sons convinced his brothers not to kill Joseph but to throw him into a pit?
    a. Judah
    b. Reuben
    c. Levi
    d. Benjamin

6. TRUE OR TRICK: Paul rebuked Peter for not eating with the Gentiles for fear of what the Jews would say.

7. FILL IN THE BLANK: Because Phinehas, Aaron's grandson, was zealous for the Lord, God gave him a covenant of an everlasting _____.

8. TRUE OR TRICK: Priscilla and Aquila were responsible for first taking the Gospel to Samaria.

9. FILL IN THE BLANK: Naaman, the leper who came to see Elisha, was captain of the army of _____.

10. FILL IN THE BLANK: The second in command to Esther's husband, King Ahasuerus, was _____.

Quiz 45
LIES AND CONSEQUENCES

Proverbs 17:20 says, "He that hath a perverse tongue falleth into mischief." What do you know about the mischief these folks got into?

1. MULTIPLE CHOICE: Elisha's servant Gehazi ran after the recently healed Syrian commander, Naaman, telling him that Elisha needed silver and garments for some unexpected guests. Gehazi's punishment for this lie was that
    a. he was struck blind
    b. he fell down dead
    c. he was given Naaman's leprosy
    d. he was consumed with fire from heaven

2. QUOTE IT: When Eve told the serpent that if they ate of the forbidden tree they would die, the serpent said. . .

3. FILL IN THE BLANK: Ananias and Sapphira, members of the early church, lied to God and their punishment was _____.

4. TRUE OR TRICK: The Lord sent a lying spirit to Ahab so the wicked king would end up doing what the Lord wanted him to do.

5. MULTIPLE CHOICE: Joseph ended up in prison as the direct result of a lie told by

    a. a slave in Potiphar's household

    b. Potiphar

    c. Potiphar's wife

    d. Pharaoh

6. TRUE OR TRICK: When Joseph's brothers sold him into slavery, they dipped his coat in goat's blood to convince their father that his favorite son was dead.

7. MULTIPLE CHOICE: When Nebuchadnezzar couldn't remember a strange dream and his wise men couldn't tell him what it was, he accused them of lying. Then he ordered that they all should be

    a. tossed in the fiery furnace

    b. slain

    c. put in the lions' den

    d. hanged

8. TRUE OR TRICK: When King Ahasuerus found out that Haman had lied about the Jews in order to destroy them, he had the man hanged on the gallows Haman had built.

9. MULTIPLE CHOICE: When King Saul lied to Samuel about destroying the Amalekites and all their possessions, Samuel knew he'd lied because of

    a. the bleating of sheep

    b. the lowing of oxen

    c. the braying of donkeys

    d. a and b

10. QUOTE IT: With Jesus on trial, when Peter was accused of following Jesus, he said, "I know not..."

Quiz 46
THE LIFE OF CHRIST

So much is written about Jesus in the Bible. How much do you know about His life here on earth?

1. TRUE OR TRICK: John is the only Gospel writer to portray Jesus weeping.

2. MULTIPLE CHOICE: When Jesus told people in the Nazareth synagogue that the prophecy of Isaiah was fulfilled in Himself, the people
    a. cheered
    b. hissed
    c. tried to throw Jesus off a cliff
    d. worshipped Him

3. TRUE OR TRICK: Jesus baptized His own disciples.

4. QUOTE IT: When a village in Samaria rejected Jesus, James and John asked Jesus, "Wilt thou that we. . ."

5. MULTIPLE CHOICE: How many women are mentioned in Jesus' genealogy in Matthew 1?
    a. none
    b. three
    c. five
    d. fourteen

6. QUOTE IT: When Jesus told the people to take the stone away from Lazarus' tomb, Martha protested saying, "Lord, by this time he stinketh. . ."

7. FILL IN THE BLANK: The woman who warned her husband to "have thou nothing to do with that just man" (Jesus) because she'd had a dream was the wife of _____.

8. TRUE OR TRICK: When Jesus sent out His twelve disciples to preach the kingdom of God, He gave them power and authority over all devils, and to cure diseases.

9. TRUE OR TRICK: Jesus sang.

10. MULTIPLE CHOICE: What town was home to Jesus' good friends Mary, Martha, and Lazarus?
    a. Bethany
    b. Bethel
    c. Bethlehem
    d. Bethsaida

Quiz 47
MED CENTER

The field of medicine is always advancing. What do you know about medicine of Bible times?

1. TRUE OR TRICK: The phrase "physician, heal thyself" is in the Bible.

2. FILL IN THE BLANK: The physician who traveled with Paul on his journeys was _____.

3. QUOTE IT: The prophet Malachi wrote that "unto you that fear [God's] name shall the Sun of righteousness. . ."

4. MULTIPLE CHOICE: God promised the Israelites that if they kept His judgments, He would take away all sickness and
    a. keep them in good health
    b. put none of the diseases of Egypt upon them
    c. would put diseases on all of Israel's enemies
    d. b and c

5. TRUE OR TRICK: King Hezekiah was once cured of an illness by applying a lump of figs to a boil.

6. MULTIPLE CHOICE: Joseph asked the physicians of Egypt to

    a. heal Jacob

    b. embalm Jacob

    c. mourn Jacob

    d. bury Jacob

7. MULTIPLE CHOICE: Which king of Judah, diseased in his feet, went to physicians for help instead of God? (By the way, he died.)

    a. Hezekiah

    b. Josiah

    c. Asa

    d. Jeroboam

8. TRUE OR TRICK: Job called his "comforters" physicians of no value.

9. MULTIPLE CHOICE: To which of the seven churches was Jesus speaking when He said He would anoint their eyes with salve to make them see?

    a. Philadelphia

    b. Ephesus

    c. Pergamos

    d. Laodicea

10. TRUE OR TRICK: Jesus once used spit to cure a blind man.

Quiz 48
MIGHTY MEN

Of course, Jesus was, is, and always will be the ultimate "Mighty Man" because He conquered the devil, sin, death, and the grave. But there are some other pretty impressive guys in the Bible. Do you know them?

1. MULTIPLE CHOICE: What judge of Israel was busy hiding his wheat from the Midianites when an angel called him a "mighty man of valour"?

    a. Abimelech

    b. Jephthah

    c. Ehud

    d. Gideon

2. TRUE OR TRICK: Even before he fought Goliath, David was referred to as a mighty and valiant man.

3. MULTIPLE CHOICE: Goliath was a huge man with huge weapons. The Bible says the staff of his spear was like a

    a. sycamore tree

    b. weaver's beam

    c. man's leg

    d. king's tent pole

4. TRUE OR TRICK: When some men tried to trap Samson by locking the gate of the city, Samson took the whole gate and carried it away.

5. TRUE OR TRICK: Caleb was sixty-five years old when he claimed his inheritance in the promised land—a mountain—and drove out three giants living there.

6. MULTIPLE CHOICE: Of whom was David speaking when he said, "How the mighty are fallen"?
    a. King Saul   c. Absalom
    b. Jonathan   d. a and b

7. MULTIPLE CHOICE: Jonathan slew twenty Philistines in their garrison with the aid of
    a. David   c. his armor-bearer
    b. his father   d. Absalom

8. MULTIPLE CHOICE: Which of the following was *not* a feat performed by one or more of David's "mighty men"?
    a. killing the brother of Goliath
    b. killing a lion in a snowy pit
    c. fetching water from a well at Bethlehem for
       David to drink
    d. killing King Saul

9. FILL IN THE BLANK: _____, a great-grandson of Noah, was known as a "mighty one in the earth" and "a mighty hunter before the LORD."

10. MULTIPLE CHOICE: Which judge of Israel killed six hundred Philistines with an ox goad?
    a. Ehud   c. Shamgar
    b. Deborah   d. Tola

Quiz 49
MIRACLES OF JESUS

Jesus refused to show the Pharisees His miraculous powers because He knew they were just trying to provoke Him. The Lord's miracles were always intended to help people. What do you know about these?

1. MULTIPLE CHOICE: Not including Himself, how many people did Jesus raise from the dead?

    a. one
    b. two
    c. three
    d. four

2. FILL IN THE BLANK: _____ is the only Gospel that records the miracle of Jesus healing a crippled man at the pool of Bethesda.

3. QUOTE IT: When Jesus calmed the sea, He said, "Peace…"

4. MULTIPLE CHOICE: After which miracle did the Pharisees begin to plot how they could destroy Jesus?

    a. healing of blind Bartimaeus
    b. healing of the woman with the issue of blood
    c. healing of the man possessed by demons
    d. healing of the man with a withered hand

5. TRUE OR TRICK: After Jesus fed the five thousand, he fed a multitude of four thousand.

6. FILL IN THE BLANK: The first public miracle Jesus performed was _____ _____ _____ _____.

7. MULTIPLE CHOICE: The last miracle Jesus performed was
     a. rising from the dead
     b. guiding His disciples to a great catch of fish
     c. walking on water
     d. withering a fig tree

8. MULTIPLE CHOICE: A coin that Peter found in a fish's mouth was
     a. given to the poor
     b. used to pay taxes
     c. spent on food
     d. deposited in the offering box at the temple

9. MULTIPLE CHOICE: When He came down from the Mount of Transfiguration, Jesus healed a boy possessed by a demon
     a. because His disciples couldn't
     b. because the boy's father begged Him
     c. because the boy was blocking His way
     d. a and b

10. FILL IN THE BLANK: When Jesus was being arrested, one of His disciples cut off the _____ of the high priest's servant—whom Jesus then healed.

Quiz 50
MIRACLES OF OTHER FOLKS

Miracles abound throughout the Bible. Although many were done by Jesus, God also performed miracles for and through other people. Would it be miraculous to get all ten of the following questions correct?

1. FILL IN THE BLANKS: The two men in the Old Testament who didn't die were _____ and _____.

2. TRUE OR TRICK: God altered time as a sign to King Hezekiah.

3. MULTIPLE CHOICE: God made the sun stand still so that Joshua and the Israelites could defeat the

    a. Philistines
    b. Edomites
    c. Moabites
    d. Amorites

4. TRUE OR TRICK: Elijah fed a hundred men with twenty loaves of bread. . .and had some left over.

5. MULTIPLE CHOICE: Which apostle actually struck someone with blindness?

    a. Matthew

    b. Peter

    c. James

    d. Paul

6. MULTIPLE CHOICE: On what mountain was Moses when he saw the burning bush?

    a. Carmel

    b. Horeb

    c. Pisgah

    d. Moriah

7. TRUE OR TRICK: A dead man fell on the bones of Joseph and was brought back to life.

8. MULTIPLE CHOICE: Which miracle was performed by both Elijah and Elisha?

    a. making an axe head float

    b. making bitter water drinkable

    c. parting the waters of the Jordan River

    d. calling down fire from heaven

9. FILL IN THE BLANK: To be cured of his leprosy, Naaman had to dip himself in the Jordan River _____ times.

10. TRUE OR TRICK: Whenever any ancient Israelite who'd been bitten by venomous snakes looked on a golden serpent Moses raised on a pole, they lived.

Quiz 51
MONEY, MONEY, MONEY

Money: some people seem to have too much of it and some people seem to have too little. What do you know about the biblical teachings on money?

1. QUOTE IT: "The love of money. . ."

2. TRUE OR TRICK: Judas Iscariot betrayed Jesus for forty pieces of silver.

3. QUOTE IT: When Pharisees tried to trap Jesus by asking Him if it was lawful to give tribute to Caesar, Jesus replied, "Render unto. . ."

4. TRUE OR TRICK: In a parable of Jesus, a servant who hid his king's money rather than conduct business with it was allowed to keep the money.

5. FILL IN THE BLANK: "The rich ruleth over the poor, and the borrower is _____ to the lender."

6. MULTIPLE CHOICE: Jesus said the widow who gave two mites gave more than the rich people because
   a. scribes and Pharisees had stolen her home
   b. she had gone to the moneychangers and been robbed
   c. their hearts were not right but her heart was
   d. they gave out of abundance and she gave all she had

7. FILL IN THE BLANK: Joseph's brothers sold him for _____ pieces of silver.

8. TRUE OR TRICK: A "penny" (or denarius) was a week's wage.

9. QUOTE IT: In the parable of the talents, the master called the servant who buried his money, "Thou wicked..."

10. TRUE OR TRICK: After Job's ordeal was over, all his brothers and sisters brought him a piece of money and a bracelet of gold.

Quiz 52
NOAH AND HIS ARK

Most people have heard of Noah and the flood. But how much do you *really* know about Noah's story?

1. TRUE OR TRICK: Noah was Methuselah's grandfather.

2. FILL IN THE BLANK: The first two animals to leave the ark were a _____ and a _____.

3. FILL IN THE BLANK: The ark was made of _____ wood.

4. TRUE OR TRICK: Only two of every kind of animal entered the ark.

5. MULTIPLE CHOICE: How old was Noah when the flood came?
  a. one hundred
  b. three hundred
  c. six hundred
  d. eight hundred

6. FILL IN THE BLANK: The number of humans on the ark was _____.

7. QUOTE IT: After all of the animals and people went aboard the ark, "the LORD. . ."

8. TRUE OR TRICK: Peter compared Noah and his ark to baptism.

9. MULTIPLE CHOICE: Jesus used the days of Noah to illustrate
    a. God's compassion
    b. the punishment of sinners
    c. the coming of the Son of Man
    d. wickedness

10. TRUE OR TRICK: Noah was on the ark for over a year.

Quiz 53
NONE LIKE GOD

Hebrews 6:13 says that "when God made promise to Abraham, because he could swear by no greater, he sware by himself." How much do you know about our unique and awesome God?

1. MULTIPLE CHOICE: To whom was God speaking when He said "that thou mayest know that there is none like me in all the earth"?

    a. Abraham

    b. David

    c. Pharaoh

    d. Jacob

2. TRUE OR TRICK: When the tabernacle was finished, the glory of the Lord filled the place and only Moses could enter.

3. MULTIPLE CHOICE: God put Elijah in a cave and revealed Himself to His prophet by

    a. an earthquake

    b. a strong wind

    c. a fire

    d. a still small voice

4. TRUE OR TRICK: Jesus is the brightness of God's glory and the express image of His person.

5. MULTIPLE CHOICE: Who was praying when she said, "There is none holy as the LORD: for there is none beside thee"?
   a. Mary, the mother of Jesus
   b. Hannah
   c. Ruth
   d. Lydia

6. QUOTE IT: Proverbs says that "the honour of kings is to search out a matter," but "it is the glory of God. . ."

7. FILL IN THE BLANK: When Jesus said, "He that hath seen me hath seen the Father," He was talking to _____.

8. TRUE OR TRICK: God said that He loved Jacob and hated Esau.

9. FILL IN THE BLANK: The book of Revelation says the seven lamps of fire burning before God's throne are the seven _____ of God.

10. QUOTE IT: "Enoch walked with God: and he was not. . ."

Quiz 54
NORTH, SOUTH, EAST, WEST

People seem to be going in all directions these days, just as they did in biblical times. What do you know about these Bible directions?

1. QUOTE IT: The star the wise men "saw in the east, went before them, till it came and. . ."

2. TRUE OR TRICK: Jesus spent most of his ministry preaching in areas south of Jerusalem.

3. FILL IN THE BLANK: The apostle Paul's call to go west to Macedonia came in a _____.

4. MULTIPLE CHOICE: Zechariah prophesied that when Jesus comes again, He will stand in the east of Jerusalem on
    a. the temple
    b. the Jordan River
    c. the Mount of Olives
    d. the necks of His enemies

5. MULTIPLE CHOICE: How many directions did God promise Jacob that his descendants would spread?

    a. one
    b. two
    c. three
    d. four

6. QUOTE IT: According to Jesus, "Many shall come from the east and west, and shall sit down with. . ."

7. FILL IN THE BLANK: God "drove out the man; and he placed at the _____ of the garden of Eden Cherubims."

8. TRUE OR TRICK: There are four gates on each wall of the new, heavenly Jerusalem.

9. MULTIPLE CHOICE: What landmark did God tell Moses marked the southern border of the promised land?

    a. the Dead Sea
    b. Mount Sinai
    c. the Red Sea
    d. the Arabian Desert

10. QUOTE IT: "For as the lightning cometh out of the east, and shineth even unto the west; so shall also. . ."

Quiz 55
O-B-E-D-I-E-N-C-E

God places a high priority on obedience to Him. What do you know about these obedient and disobedient biblical folks?

1. MULTIPLE CHOICE: When Barak hesitated to obey God's command to fight the army of Sisera, Deborah the judge told Barak that. . .

    a. he would die in battle

    b. the Israelites would lose to Sisera

    c. Deborah herself would die in the conflict

    d. a woman would kill Sisera

2. QUOTE IT: When the Jewish high priest and council told Jesus' apostles not to preach any more, Peter and the other apostles replied, "We ought. . ."

3. MULTIPLE CHOICE: Shadrach, Meshach, and Abednego were thrown into the fiery furnace when they refused to disobey God by

    a. kneeling before Nebuchadnezzar

    b. burning incense to Nebuchadnezzar's gods

    c. bowing to a golden statue

    d. praying to Nebuchadnezzar's wise men

4. FILL IN THE BLANK: When King Saul disobeyed the Lord by not completely destroying the Amalekites, Samuel told him that "to obey is better than _____."

5. QUOTE IT: When the angel Gabriel told Mary that she was to be the mother of Jesus, Mary replied, "Behold the handmaid of the Lord. . ."

6. MULTIPLE CHOICE: When Mordecai persuaded Esther to risk her own life to save her people, Esther replied,
    a. "Fast ye for me"
    b. "If I perish, I perish"
    c. "I will go if you go with me"
    d. a and b

7. TRUE OR TRICK: Daniel deliberately defied King Darius's order by praying with his windows open, three times a day.

8. FILL IN THE BLANK: In obedience to God, Abraham took Isaac to Mount _____ to offer him as a sacrifice.

9. QUOTE IT: "Wherefore, my beloved, as ye have always obeyed, not as in my presence only, but now much more in my absence, work out. . ."

10. FILL IN THE BLANK: "And all these _____ shall come on thee, and overtake thee, if thou shalt hearken unto the voice of the LORD thy God."

Quiz 56
OLD FOLKS

Scripture contains the stories of many old folks—some *really* old folks. What do you know about them?

1. FILL IN THE BLANK: "Old as Methuselah" is a common phrase. Methuselah lived _____ years.

2. TRUE OR TRICK: Anna was a ninety-four-year-old prophetess who stayed in the temple day and night waiting for Messiah to come.

3. QUOTE IT: Toward the end of his life, Joshua called for the people of Israel and their leaders and said, "I am old and..."

4. MULTIPLE CHOICE: Sarah was ninety when she gave birth to Isaac and _____ when she died.
    a. 100
    b. 117
    c. 127
    d. 137

5. MULTIPLE CHOICE: Which prophet referred to the Lord as "the Ancient of Days"?
  a. Isaiah
  b. Ezekiel
  c. Daniel
  d. Zechariah

6. FILL IN THE BLANK: Noah was _____ when Shem, Ham, and Japheth were born.

7. MULTIPLE CHOICE: Of whom was it said, when he died at 120, that "his eye was not dim, nor his natural force abated"?
  a. Aaron
  b. Abraham
  c. Moses
  d. David

8. TRUE OR TRICK: Adam lived over nine hundred years.

9. QUOTE IT: "Thou shalt rise up before the..."

10. TRUE OR TRICK: Enoch was 365 years old when he died.

Quiz 57
OLIVES

Ever realized how often *olives* are mentioned in the Bible? See what you can recall of this very important edible!

1. MULTIPLE CHOICE: Which of the following was *not* a spice mixed with olive oil to make the anointing oil for priests?

    a. cinnamon
    b. myrrh
    c. cassia
    d. cummin

2. QUOTE IT: When Noah sent a dove from the ark, "the dove came in to him in the evening; and, lo. . ."

3. TRUE OR TRICK: The garden of Gethsemane was located on the Mount of Olives.

4. FILL IN THE BLANK: Regarding the lamps in the tabernacle, God told Moses, "Command the children of Israel, that they bring unto thee pure oil olive beaten for the light, to cause the lamps to burn _____."

5. MULTIPLE CHOICE: The prophet who prophesied that in the day of the Lord the Mount of Olives will split down the middle is
- a. Zephaniah
- b. Daniel
- c. Ezekiel
- d. Zechariah

6. TRUE OR TRICK: When the Queen of Sheba visited Solomon, one of the gifts she brought him was a hundred pounds of olives.

7. MULTIPLE CHOICE: Which book of the Bible says if a man walks in the ways of the Lord his children will be like olive plants around his table?
- a. Psalms
- b. Proverbs
- c. Ecclesiastes
- d. Job

8. FILL IN THE BLANKS: When Paul said, "Thou, being a wild olive tree, wert grafted in. . ." he was referring to
_____ _____.

9. TRUE OR TRICK: When Jesus was transfigured He was on the Mount of Olives.

10. QUOTE IT: God told the Israelites that He would make them desolate because of their sins: "Thou shalt sow, but thou shalt not reap; thou shalt tread the olives..."

Quiz 58
PEOPLE TO SEE

Beauty, they say, is in the eye of the beholder. Sometimes beauty is skin deep. What do you know about these biblical beauties—some inwardly, some outwardly?

1. MULTIPLE CHOICE: Whose wife was so beautiful that he said she was his sister because he was afraid the men of the land would kill him and take her?

    a. Abraham

    b. Isaac

    c. Jacob

    d. a and b

2. MULTIPLE CHOICE: In all of Israel "there was none to be so much praised" for his beauty as Absalom. Every year he

    a. took a bath in rich perfumes and ointments

    b. had a ceremony to show himself arrayed in costly garments

    c. cut his hair and weighed it

    d. took another wife

3. FILL IN THE BLANK: Rachel was beautiful and well favored but Leah was _____.

4. TRUE OR TRICK: The saying "beauty is in the eye of the beholder" is in the Bible.

5. FILL IN THE BLANK: The beautiful queen who refused to let her husband show her off to all his drunken nobles was _____.

6. QUOTE IT: "In all the land were no women found so fair as. . ."

7. FILL IN THE BLANK: The beautiful woman spied on while she was bathing was _____.

8. MULTIPLE CHOICE: In the Song of Solomon, which of the following is *not* among the lover's compliments of his bride's beauty?
    a. "thy navel is like a round goblet"
    b. "the toes of thy feet like pebbles"
    c. "thy neck is as a tower of ivory"
    d. "the hair of thine head like purple"

9. FILL IN THE BLANK: The wise and beautiful Abigail, wife of King David, was widow of the churlish and evil _____.

10. QUOTE IT: "Ye wives. . . . whose adorning let it not be that outward adorning of plaiting the hair, and of wearing of gold, or of putting on of apparel; but let it be the hidden man of the heart, in that which is not corruptible, even the ornament of. . ."

Quiz 59
PLACES TO BE

The Bible is full of real people, real events, and real places. What do you know of the following locales?

1. FILL IN THE BLANK: King Saul disobeyed God by consulting a witch at _____.

2. TRUE OR TRICK: David was anointed king at Hebron.

3. MULTIPLE CHOICE: The Bible's first mention of the name *Jerusalem* is in
    a. Genesis
    b. Leviticus
    c. Deuteronomy
    d. Joshua

4. TRUE OR TRICK: The beat-up traveler helped by the Good Samaritan was on his way to Jericho.

5. QUOTE IT: The prophet Micah says that out of Bethlehem will come a "ruler in Israel. . ."

6. FILL IN THE BLANK: Jesus spoke to the woman at the well in _____.

7. MULTIPLE CHOICE: Before the temple was built in Jerusalem, the house of God and the ark of the covenant were in

    a. Bethel

    b. Bethlehem

    c. Shiloh

    d. Gilgal

8. FILL IN THE BLANK: God confounded the language of the earth at the tower of _____.

9. TRUE OR TRICK: Moses both received the Ten Commandments and saw the promised land on Mount Sinai.

10. MULTIPLE CHOICE: Toward the end of his life, Jeremiah was taken captive to what country?

    a. Babylon

    b. Assyria

    c. Egypt

    d. Edom

Quiz 60
PLAY ME A SONG

Human beings sing all kinds of songs. In Bible times, many of them were praises to God. What do you know about the following songs?

1. TRUE OR TRICK: The first song in the Bible and the last song in the Bible were written by Moses.

2. MULTIPLE CHOICE: What object did the Israelites sing a song to in the wilderness?
    a. the brass snake on a pole
    b. a rock
    c. the pillar of cloud
    d. a well

3. FILL IN THE BLANK: "The horse and his rider hath he thrown into the sea," was part of a song sung by Moses' sister, _____.

4. TRUE OR TRICK: The longest book in the Bible is a book of songs.

5. MULTIPLE CHOICE: According to the book of Ecclesiastes, what is better than to "hear the song of fools"?

    a. "to hear the rebuke of the wise"

    b. "to hear the preaching of God's Word"

    c. "to hear the voice of the Teacher"

    d. "to hear the trumpet call to battle"

6. TRUE OR TRICK: King Saul got jealous of David because of a song some women sang.

7. QUOTE IT: According to a psalm writer, God "hath put a new song. . ."

8. MULTIPLE CHOICE: Someone who sings songs to a person with a heavy heart is like

    a. vinegar poured on soda

    b. opening a wound

    c. a pig with a gold ring in its snout

    d. an angel singing

9. QUOTE IT: The book of Ephesians says to sing and "make melody. . ."

10. MULTIPLE CHOICE: Job's friend Elihu said that God gives songs

    a. in the night

    b. in dire circumstances

    c. when you trust Him

    d. when your enemies are defeated

Quiz 61
PROPHETS AND PROPHECIES

Moses prophesied that God would send a "prophet like unto me" which, of course, was Jesus. What do you know about these other prophets and prophetesses?

1. MULTIPLE CHOICE: Which prophet referred to his wife as a prophetess?
　　a. Ezekiel
　　b. Hosea
　　c. Jeremiah
　　d. Isaiah

2. QUOTE IT: The very last prophecy in the Bible says, "Surely. . ."

3. FILL IN THE BLANKS: Jesus said the greatest prophet that was born of woman was _____ _____ _____.

4. FILL IN THE BLANKS: The prophets who appeared on the mountain when Jesus was transfigured were _____ and _____.

5. TRUE OR TRICK: There was a prophetess named Jezebel.

6. MULTIPLE CHOICE: The prophecy concerning a city to be named "The LORD Is There" was made by

    a. Daniel

    b. John

    c. Ezekiel

    d. Zechariah

7. TRUE OR TRICK: Moses' sister, Miriam, was a prophetess.

8. FILL IN THE BLANK: The prophecy "a virgin shall conceive, and bear a son, and shall call his name Immanuel" was recorded by _____.

9. TRUE OR TRICK: King Saul prophesied among the prophets.

10. QUOTE IT: When God cursed the serpent in the Garden of Eden, He made a prophecy, saying the woman's seed would bruise the serpent's head and the serpent "shalt bruise. . ."

Quiz 62
QUAILS AND OTHER FOWL

The Lord once used quails to punish the Israelites for all their complaining in the wilderness (Numbers 11:18–20). What do you know about these other biblical fowl?

1. TRUE OR TRICK: Swans were considered to be unclean animals to the Israelites and not to be eaten.

2. FILL IN THE BLANK: The most well-known story involving a rooster (or cock) is closely associated with _____.

3. TRUE OR TRICK: Although a rooster (or cock) is mentioned in the Bible, there is no mention of a hen or chickens.

4. FILL IN THE BLANK: The first bird Noah sent off the ark was a _____.

5. QUOTE IT: "Behold the fowls of the air: for they sow not, neither do they reap, nor gather into barns; yet. . ."

6. FILL IN THE BLANK: When Elijah was hiding from King Ahab by the brook Cherith, God sent _____ to feed him.

7. QUOTE IT: When Jesus was baptized, the heavens were opened unto Him, "and he saw the Spirit of God…"

8. MULTIPLE CHOICE: To what type of bird was Jesus referring when He said that not one of them is forgotten before God?

    a. raven
    b. dove
    c. sparrow
    d. wren

9. MULTIPLE CHOICE: Which of the following birds was *not* considered to be unclean and therefore forbidden as food to the Israelites?

    a. stork
    b. owl
    c. pelican
    d. none of the above—all were unclean

10. FILL IN THE BLANK: Isaiah 40:31 says "they that wait upon the LORD shall renew their strength; they shall mount up with wings as _____."

Quiz 63
RABBI! RABBI!

Many people brought questions to Jesus. Some were genuinely curious and some were just trying to trick Him. Can you tell which is which?

1. MULTIPLE CHOICE: When asked "who is my neighbor?" Jesus responded with the parable of
    a. the prodigal son
    b. the sower and the seed
    c. the good Samaritan
    d. the lost sheep

2. TRUE OR TRICK: Nicodemus asked Jesus, "What shall I do that I may inherit eternal life?"

3. MULTIPLE CHOICE: When John the Baptist told two of his disciples, "Behold the Lamb of God," those disciples went to Jesus and asked, "Rabbi. . ."
    a. "mayest we follow thou?"
    b. "canst thou feed us?"
    c. "where dwellest thou?"
    d. "art thou the Messiah?"

4. MULTIPLE CHOICE: Who asked Jesus, "Is it lawful for a man to put away his wife for every cause?"

    a. Peter

    b. the Sadducees

    c. the Pharisees

    d. Philip

5. QUOTE IT: At a wedding in Cana, when Mary urged Jesus to do something about the wine, He replied, "Mine hour. . ."

6. QUOTE IT: When Paul, on the road to Damascus, asked, "Who art thou, Lord?" Jesus replied, "I am Jesus. . ."

7. MULTIPLE CHOICE: Who asked Jesus, "What have I to do with thee, Jesus, thou Son of the most high God?"

    a. a man possessed of many devils

    b. Satan

    c. a Pharisee

    d. a scribe

8. TRUE OR TRICK: The two men on the road to Emmaus who walked and talked with the resurrected Jesus never knew who He was.

9. FILL IN THE BLANK: When the Pharisees demanded that Jesus show them a sign from heaven, Jesus replied that the only sign they would be given was the sign of the prophet _____.

10. FILL IN THE BLANK: When Jesus asked, "Whom say ye that I am?" _____ replied, "Thou art the Christ, the Son of the living God."

Quiz 64
REDEEMED, HOW I LOVE TO PROCLAIM IT

Redeemed means ransomed, recovered, rescued, restored. While it especially applies to salvation, the word was used in other biblical contexts as well. What do you know about these?

1. MULTIPLE CHOICE: To whom did Jesus say, "Thy faith hath made thee whole; go in peace"?
   a. a man with a sick servant
   b. a centurion with a sick son
   c. a woman with an issue of blood
   d. the synagogue leader Jairus

2. FILL IN THE BLANK: An Ethiopian _____ accepted Jesus as Lord with the help of Philip on a desert road.

3. TRUE OR TRICK: Cornelius was a devout Gentile saved through the witness of Paul.

4. MULTIPLE CHOICE: To whom was Jesus speaking when He said, "This day is salvation come to this house"?
   a. the bridegroom at Cana
   b. Peter's mother-in-law
   c. Zacchaeus
   d. Simon the Leper

5. TRUE OR TRICK: There was a kinsman closer than Boaz who had the first right to redeem Elimelech's land and marry Ruth.

6. TRUE OR TRICK: In the year of Jubilee, Jewish people who had been sold into servitude were given a chance to be redeemed by family members.

7. QUOTE IT: Job said, "I know that my redeemer liveth, and that he shall stand. . ."

8. FILL IN THE BLANK: According to the apostle Paul's letter to the Colossians, we have redemption through Jesus' _____.

9. QUOTE IT: "Redeeming the time. . ."

10. FILL IN THE BLANK: "Neither by the blood of goats and calves, but by his own blood [Jesus] entered in once into the holy place, having obtained _____ redemption for us."

Quiz 65
RICHES, FALSE AND TRUE

Jesus said, "You cannot serve God and mammon." *Mammon* was a term for riches. What do you know about true and false riches?

1. TRUE OR TRICK: The apostle John quoted Jesus as saying, "Ye cannot serve God and mammon."

2. QUOTE IT: "Lay up for yourselves treasures in heaven, where neither moth nor rust doth corrupt, and where. . ."

3. TRUE OR TRICK: Solomon had so much gold that silver was worth nothing in his kingdom.

4. QUOTE IT: When Jesus said it was easier for a camel to go through the eye of a needle than for a rich man to enter the kingdom of God, His disciples were "exceedingly amazed, saying. . ."

5. TRUE OR TRICK: The Bible says riches can make themselves wings and fly away.

6. TRUE OR TRICK: When Jesus told a rich young ruler to sell everything he had, give it to the poor, and follow Him, the man did it gladly.

7. MULTIPLE CHOICE: How did the apostle Paul describe the "riches of Christ" to believers in Ephesus?

    a. unsearchable
    b. effusive
    c. almighty
    d. never-ending

8. MULTIPLE CHOICE: In the parable of the rich fool, God called the prosperous man foolish because. . .

    a. he was boasting about his riches
    b. his soul would be required of him that night
    c. he didn't have enough room to store his riches
    d. he said, "eat, drink and be merry"

9. MULTIPLE CHOICE: Which of the seven churches of Asia Minor did Jesus counsel to buy from Him "gold tried in the fire" that they might be rich?

    a. Philadelphia
    b. Pergamos
    c. Smyrna
    d. Laodicea

10. TRUE OR TRICK: After all Job's sufferings, the Lord gave him ten times as much as he'd had before.

Quiz 66
THE RESURRECTION

Christ died for our sins according to the scriptures, and He was buried and rose again according to the scriptures (1 Corinthians 15:3–4). What do you recall about this most significant idea?

1. FILL IN THE BLANK: When Jesus said, "I am the resurrection and the life" He was speaking to _____.

2. QUOTE IT: The women who came to the tomb early on the morning of the third day asked themselves, "Who shall. . ."

3. TRUE OR TRICK: When an angel rolled the stone away from the tomb, there was a great wind.

4. FILL IN THE BLANKS: The angels at the tomb asked the women, "Why seek ye the _____ among the _____?"

5. MULTIPLE CHOICE: When Peter entered Jesus' tomb, it was empty except for
    a. Mary Magdalene
    b. the linen cloths
    c. an angel
    d. Roman soldiers

6. QUOTE IT: When the women ran and told the disciples that Jesus had risen, "their words seemed to them as idle tales, and. . ."

7. MULTIPLE CHOICE: When the chief priests and elders learned about the empty tomb, what did they do to the soldiers who were guarding it?
    a. sent them to a far country
    b. put them in prison
    c. beat them and commanded them not to speak of the matter
    d. gave them money

8. TRUE OR TRICK: When the disciples gathered together after the resurrection, Jesus appeared in their midst in spite of locked doors.

9. TRUE OR TRICK: The disciple Bartholomew demanded to see the nail prints in Jesus' hands and side.

10. MULTIPLE CHOICE: Jesus was near which city when He ascended back into heaven?
    a. Jerusalem
    b. Bethlehem
    c. Bethany
    d. Jericho

Quiz 67
SAYINGS OF JESUS

Jesus taught His disciples and many other people while He was on earth. What do you recall about what He said?

1. QUOTE IT: In a sermon about the coming of God's kingdom, Jesus spoke a very short verse: "Remember. . ."

2. TRUE OR TRICK: Jesus said a prophet is honored anywhere except his own country and in his own house.

3. MULTIPLE CHOICE: To whom was Jesus speaking when He said, "That thou doest, do quickly"?
    a. Zacchaeus
    b. Peter
    c. the rich young ruler
    d. Judas Iscariot

4. QUOTE IT: When the Pharisees tried to trick Jesus by asking if it was lawful to give tribute to Caesar, the Lord replied, "Render therefore unto Caesar the things which are Caesar's. . ."

5. FILL IN THE BLANK: Jesus asked, "Where have ye laid him?" about _____.

6. MULTIPLE CHOICE: Jesus said, "Woman, why weepest thou?" to

    a. His mother

    b. the woman at the well

    c. Lazarus' sister, Mary

    d. Mary Magdalene

7. QUOTE IT: After the resurrection, Jesus asked three times if Peter loved Him. Hurt, Peter finally replied, "Lord, thou knowest that I love thee." Jesus replied. . .

8. FILL IN THE BLANK: When Jesus said, "I am Alpha and Omega, the beginning and the ending" He was speaking to _____.

9. MULTIPLE CHOICE: To whom was Jesus speaking when He said, "Do ye not therefore err, because ye know not the scriptures, neither the power of God?"

    a. Pharisees

    b. Sadducees

    c. scribes

    d. all of the above

10. TRUE OR TRICK: Jesus said that the end of the world would not come until the gospel of the kingdom was preached to all nations.

Quiz 68
SCRIPTURE ON SCRIPTURE

How much do you know about what the Bible says of itself?

1. QUOTE IT: "All scripture is given by inspiration of God, and is profitable for doctrine, for reproof, for correction. . ."

2. MULTIPLE CHOICE: God says His Word will not return to Him void but will
    a. accomplish what He pleases
    b. bless all nations
    c. prosper in the thing He sent it to do
    d. a and c

3. MULTIPLE CHOICE: To whom was the angel Michael speaking when he said he would show him what was in the "scripture of truth"?
    a. John
    b. Elijah
    c. Peter
    d. Daniel

4. QUOTE IT: "Thy word have I hid in mine heart, that I might not. . ."

5. TRUE OR TRICK: The Bible calls itself the "holy scriptures."

6. FILL IN THE BLANKS: The word of God is quick and powerful and sharper than any _____ _____.

7. QUOTE IT: In the armor of God listed in Ephesians 6, the word of God is described as "the. . ."

8. MULTIPLE CHOICE: "For ever, O LORD, thy word is settled in heaven" is written in
    a. Isaiah
    b. Zechariah
    c. Psalms
    d. Proverbs

9. TRUE OR TRICK: The Bible calls Jesus "the Word of God."

10. MULTIPLE CHOICE: Jesus said, "Search the scriptures; for in them ye think ye have eternal life: and they are they. . ."
    a. "by which ye live"
    b. "which testify of me"
    c. "which are spoken by God"
    d. "which bring eternal life"

Quiz 69
SERVANTS ALL

Jesus is the perfect servant who knew His duty to God the Father and performed it completely. We are called to serve as well. Can you serve up the answers to these questions?

1. MULTIPLE CHOICE: Ecclesiastes says the "whole duty of man" is to

    a. "love the Lord your God with all your mind, heart and strength"

    b. "fear God and keep His commandments"

    c. "trust in the Lord with all your heart"

    d. all of the above

2. FILL IN THE BLANK: Jesus made Himself of no reputation and became a servant because He "thought it not _____ to be equal with God."

3. QUOTE IT: Jesus "endured the cross, despising the shame, and is set down at the right hand of the throne of God" because of "the joy. . ."

4. MULTIPLE CHOICE: We are to present our bodies as living sacrifices, holy and acceptable unto God, which is our _____ service.

    a. responsible   c. reasonable

    b. required   d. rational

5. QUOTE IT: When Jesus was twelve and Mary and Joseph found Him in the temple, He told them, "How is it that ye sought me? wist ye not that I..."

6. MULTIPLE CHOICE: Withhold no good from them to whom it is due...

    a. unless they are evil

    b. before thou hast prayed

    c. until God has spoken

    d. when it is in your power to do it

7. QUOTE IT: "The disciple is not above his master..."

8. MULTIPLE CHOICE: To which church of Asia Minor did Jesus say, "I know thy works, and charity, and service, and faith"?

    a. Thyatira   c. Philadelphia

    b. Smyrna   d. Pergamos

9. FILL IN THE BLANK: "Keep back thy servant also from _____ sins."

10. QUOTE IT: At the end of time, on the new earth, "there shall be no more curse: but the throne of God and of the Lamb shall be in it; and his servants..."

Quiz 70
SHADOW OF DEATH

Death is inevitable, but the thought of is frightening to the vast majority of people. What do you remember of what the Bible says about death?

1. QUOTE IT: "Precious in the sight of the LORD is the death. . ."

2. FILL IN THE BLANK: The phrase, "the valley of the shadow of death" is found in Psalm _____.

3. TRUE OR TRICK: Passover gets its name from the angel of death passing over the Israelite houses with blood on their doorposts.

4. QUOTE IT: "There is a way which seemeth right unto a man. . ."

5. MULTIPLE CHOICE: Revelation describes the second death as
  a. the great white throne judgment
  b. when the sea gives up its dead
  c. when the angel declares that time will be no more
  d. when death and hell are cast into the lake of fire

6. TRUE OR TRICK: Jesus gave Peter a hint at the kind of death he would die.

7. MULTIPLE CHOICE: God healed a king who was sick unto death and added fifteen years to that king's life. That king was
    a. David
    b. Saul
    c. Hezekiah
    d. Jehoshaphat

8. TRUE OR TRICK: When Abraham died, Isaac and Ishmael, his sons by different mothers, buried him next to Sarah.

9. FILL IN THE BLANK: Just before Jesus died on the cross, darkness covered the earth for _____ hours.

10. QUOTE IT: "O death, where is thy sting? O grave..."

Quiz 71
SHEEP AND THE SHEPHERD

Sheep need constant attention and tend to wander off. How do you feel being known as a sheep? Just never forget that Jesus Himself is the Shepherd!

1. FILL IN THE BLANK: When Jesus returns in His glory, He will separate the people of earth as a shepherd divides his sheep from the _____.

2. QUOTE IT: Jesus said, "I am the good shepherd: the good shepherd giveth. . ."

3. MULTIPLE CHOICE: Which of the following scriptures does *not* say we are like sheep going astray?
    a. 1 Peter 2:25
    b. Isaiah 53:6
    c. Psalm 119:176
    d. Psalm 100:3

4. FILL IN THE BLANK: The book of Hebrews calls Jesus the _____ shepherd of the sheep.

5. TRUE OR TRICK: Jesus says He calls His own sheep by name.

6. MULTIPLE CHOICE: In addition to being the shepherd, Jesus also said he was the _____ of the sheep.
   a. leader
   b. head
   c. door
   d. king

7. TRUE OR TRICK: Jesus told six parables about sheep.

8. TRUE OR TRICK: The Lord leads us in the paths of righteousness for our own sake.

9. MULTIPLE CHOICE: Which of Jesus' disciples called Him the chief Shepherd?
   a. Peter
   b. Andrew
   c. James
   d. Paul

10. QUOTE IT: In addition to being our shepherd, Jesus is also "the Lamb of God, which. . ."

Quiz 72
SIMON PETER

Like many of us, Peter had his ups and downs when it came to his faith in Jesus. What do you know about this impetuous apostle?

1. FILL IN THE BLANK: When Peter preached his sermon on Pentecost, he specifically quoted the prophet _____.

2. MULTIPLE CHOICE: On the mount of transfiguration, Peter
    a. wanted to worship God
    b. was struck dumb
    c. fell down as if dead
    d. wanted to build three tabernacles

3. TRUE OR TRICK: When women told the disciples that Jesus' tomb was empty, Peter outran John to the burial site.

4. MULTIPLE CHOICE: Jesus called Peter out of the boat to walk on water to Him. However, Peter began to sink when he saw _____ and became afraid.
    a. the waves
    b. what he thought was a ghost
    c. the wind
    d. the rocks too close to the boat

5. TRUE OR TRICK: The only time the word *Easter* appears in the King James Bible is in connection with Peter.

6. FILL IN THE BLANK: After the resurrection, Jesus asked Peter _____ times if Peter loved Him.

7. TRUE OR TRICK: On the night of Jesus' arrest, Peter was praying with Him in Gethsemane.

8. FILL IN THE BLANK: Peter wrote _____ books of the Bible.

9. TRUE OR TRICK: Peter was the only one of Jesus' twelve disciples actually named Simon.

10. MULTIPLE CHOICE: What relative of Peter was healed of a fever by Jesus?
    a. his wife
    b. his son
    c. his mother-in-law
    d. a cousin

Quiz 73
SIN, UGH

"For all have sinned, and come short of the glory of God" (Romans 3:23). What do you know about sin and its consequences?

1. QUOTE IT: "For the wages of sin is death; but the gift of God is. . ."

2. FILL IN THE BLANK: A lying tongue is an _____ to the Lord.

3. TRUE OR TRICK: Ananias and Syntyche both lied to the Holy Spirit and both fell down dead.

4. FILL IN THE BLANK: God occasionally destroyed cities because their sins were so great. The two most famous were from Abraham's day: _____ and _____.

5. MULTIPLE CHOICE: Though he should have been warned when his donkey miraculously spoke, Balaam insisted on disobeying God. The punishment for his sin was
    a. he fell off a mountain
    b. he was taken captive
    c. he was killed by Moses' command
    d. he was killed by the king of Moab

6. QUOTE IT: "To him that knoweth to do good, and doeth it not. . ."

7. MULTIPLE CHOICE: Miriam and Aaron spoke against Moses, saying that they were prophets as much as he was. The Lord rebuked them and struck Miriam with leprosy for
   a. the rest of her days
   b. seven days
   c. a year
   d. a day

8. MULTIPLE CHOICE: According to the Psalms, how far has God removed our sin from us?
   a. as far as the north is from the south
   b. as far as the east is from the west
   c. as far as heaven is from hell
   d. as far as the earth is from the sun

9. QUOTE IT: "If we confess our sins, he is faithful and just to forgive us our sins, and. . ."

10. TRUE OR TRICK: The Bible says you can be angry and not sin.

Quiz 74
SOLDIERY

We are part of God's army, but the enemies we fight today are not physical. In Bible times, they often were. What do you know about these armies and soldiers?

1. MULTIPLE CHOICE: What nation's king besieged Israel, went to sleep, and upon waking found his entire army dead?
    a. Moab
    b. Midian
    c. Assyria
    d. Edom

2. TRUE OR TRICK: David got to marry King Saul's daughter by fighting against the Midianites.

3. FILL IN THE BLANK: Because he had told the Persian king that God would protect the Jews, the prophet _____ was ashamed to ask Artaxerxes for a military escort.

4. MULTIPLE CHOICE: For what king did God use singers instead of armies to defeat the Moabites and Ammonites?
    a. Rehoboam
    b. Abijah
    c. Hezekiah
    d. Jehoshaphat

5. FILL IN THE BLANK: Gideon's army originally had thirty-two thousand men but he ended up with an army of _____.

6. QUOTE IT: David told Goliath, "Thou comest to me with a sword, and with a spear, and with a shield: but I come to thee. . ."

7. TRUE OR TRICK: The prophet Elisha prayed for his servant to see God's invisible spiritual army.

8. MULTIPLE CHOICE: When the Philistines stole the ark of the covenant, what did they do with it?
   a. put it in the house of their god, Dagon
   b. returned it to Israel
   c. opened it and looked inside
   d. a and b

9. MULTIPLE CHOICE: How did God keep David, living among the Philistines while he ran from King Saul, from being pressed into a fight against the Israelites?
   a. He made David a madman
   b. He turned Philistine commanders against him so they wouldn't let him fight
   c. He made the Philistine soothsayers predict failure if David fought with them
   d. He struck David with leprosy

10. FILL IN THE BLANK: The Jews who rebuilt Jerusalem's wall under the leadership of Nehemiah worked with one hand "and with the other hand held a _____."

Quiz 75
SOLOMON SAYS

According to scripture, Solomon "spake three thousand proverbs: and his songs were a thousand and five" (1 Kings 4:32) What else do you know about this very wise king's teaching?

1. FILL IN THE BLANKS: "_____ of _____, saith the Preacher. . .all is _____."

2. TRUE OR TRICK: Solomon said, "A little bird told me."

3. MULTIPLE CHOICE: "Dead flies cause the ointment of the apothecary to send forth a stinking savour: so doth a little _____ him that is in reputation for wisdom and honour."
    a. deceit
    b. folly
    c. sin
    d. falsehood

4. QUOTE IT: "The fear of the LORD is. . ."

5. TRUE OR TRICK: Solomon said pride goes before a fall.

6. TRUE OR TRICK: Solomon said if you play with fire you will get burned.

7. MULTIPLE CHOICE: Two are better than one because
   a. they have a good reward for their labor
   b. if they fall one will lift up his fellow
   c. if they lie together they will be warm
   d. all of the above

8. FILL IN THE BLANK: "Many waters cannot quench
_____."

9. QUOTE IT: "Trust in the LORD with all thine heart;
and lean not unto thine own understanding. In all thy
ways acknowledge him. . ."

10. MULTIPLE CHOICE: The Lord will make a man's
enemies be at peace with him when
   a. the man asks for help
   b. the man prays
   c. the man's ways please the Lord
   d. the man treats his children well

Quiz 76
SOWING, REAPING

"Be not deceived; God is not mocked: for whatsoever a man soweth, that shall he also reap." (Galatians 6:7) What do you know about this powerful biblical principle?

1. MULTIPLE CHOICE: What was Jesus describing when He urged people to consider them that "sow not, neither do they reap"?

    a. the lilies of the field
    b. the fish of the sea
    c. the fowls of the air
    d. little children

2. FILL IN THE BLANK: "He that soweth to his flesh shall of the flesh reap _____; but he that soweth to the Spirit shall of the Spirit reap _____."

3. TRUE OR TRICK: The Bible says sowing the wind means reaping the whirlwind.

4. FILL IN THE BLANK: The ancient Israelites were to sow their field for _____ years and then let them lie fallow for one.

5. MULTIPLE CHOICE: In the fiftieth year, the Israelites were to neither sow nor reap. This was called the year of
   a. fasting
   b. Sabbath
   c. glory to the Lord
   d. Jubilee

6. FILL IN THE BLANK: "They that sow in _____ shall reap in _____."

7. FILL IN THE BLANK: "He that soweth iniquity shall reap _____."

8. MULTIPLE CHOICE: "_____ is sown for the righteous, and _____ for the upright in heart."
   a. joy, rejoicing
   b. light, gladness
   c. love, faith
   d. joy, faith

9. FILL IN THE BLANKS: "He that observeth the _____ shall not sow; and he that regardeth the _____ shall not reap."

10. QUOTE IT: "He which soweth sparingly shall reap also sparingly..."

Quiz 77
SUFFERING'S BRIGHT SIDE

Jesus told His disciples, "In the world ye shall have tribulation: but be of good cheer; I have overcome the world" (John 16:33). God has promised to bless us in our trials. What do you know about these blessings?

1. QUOTE IT: "When thou passest through the waters. . ."

2. MULTIPLE CHOICE: To which of the seven churches did Jesus promise, "To him that overcometh will I give to eat of the tree of life"?
    a. Philadelphia
    b. Thyatira
    c. Smyrna
    d. Ephesus

3. QUOTE IT: After Jacob's death, Joseph told his brothers, "Ye thought evil against me; but God. . ."

4. QUOTE IT: "Fear thou not; for I am with thee: be not dismayed; for I am thy God; I will strengthen thee; yea, I will help thee; yea, I will. . ."

5. FILL IN THE BLANK: The apostle Peter wrote that suffering for _____ sake will make a person happy.

6. MULTIPLE CHOICE: Of which of his sons did Jacob say, "The archers have sorely grieved him. . .but the God of his fathers shall bless him"?

    a. Judah

    b. Benjamin

    c. Levi

    d. Joseph

7. MULTIPLE CHOICE: "Yea, though I walk through the valley of the shadow of death, I will fear no evil..."

    a. "for thou art with me"

    b. "thy rod and thy staff they comfort me"

    c. "thou restorest my soul"

    d. a and b

8. FILL IN THE BLANK: The apostle Paul said he was "persecuted, but not _____."

9. QUOTE IT: "The Lord is my helper, and I will not fear. . ."

10. TRUE OR TRICK: Though our outward man perish, yet our inward man is renewed moment by moment.

Quiz 78
TABERNACLE AND TEMPLE

God "admonished" Moses to make the tabernacle according to the pattern he'd received on Mount Sinai (Hebrews 8:5). Later, David and his son Solomon made a permanent temple for the Israelites. What do you know about these places of worship?

1. MULTIPLE CHOICE: The two men to whom God gave wisdom, understanding, and knowledge "in all manner of workmanship" for building the tabernacle were
    a. Nadab and Abihu
    b. Dathan and Korah
    c. Bezaleel and Aholiab
    d. Huz and Buz

2. QUOTE IT: When the tabernacle was finished, "a cloud covered the tent of the congregation..."

3. FILL IN THE BLANKS: The furnishings of the tabernacle included an altar for burnt offerings, a laver, a table of shewbread, a lampstand, an altar of incense, and the

_____ _____ _____ _____.

4. FILL IN THE BLANK: The tribe given the task of dismantling, transporting, and reassembling the tabernacle each time the Israelites broke camp was the tribe of _____.

5. MULTIPLE CHOICE: When the tabernacle was finished, God told Moses to anoint it with

    a. pure olive oil

    b. a spiced oil ointment

    c. ram's blood

    d. water from the rock

6. TRUE OR TRICK: David wanted to build the temple but God told him he couldn't.

7. TRUE OR TRICK: Solomon was the only builder of the Jerusalem temple.

8. QUOTE IT: When God's glory filled the temple that Solomon built, the people "bowed themselves with their faces to the ground upon the pavement, and worshipped, and praised the LORD, saying, For he is good; for his mercy. . ."

9. MULTIPLE CHOICE: How many years had the temple of Jesus' day been under construction?

    a. ten

    b. thirteen

    c. twenty-seven

    d. forty-six

10. MULTIPLE CHOICE: The last person on earth to see the ark of the covenant was

    a. Jeremiah

    b. Ezekiel

    c. Daniel

    d. John

Quiz 79
TAXED ENOUGH ALREADY

Taxes are nothing new. Neither are grumbling and grousing against them. What do you know about biblical taxes and tax collectors?

1. FILL IN THE BLANK: The disciple of Jesus who was a tax collector was _____.

2. TRUE OR TRICK: Joseph and Mary went to Bethlehem because "all the world" was being taxed.

3. FILL IN THE BLANK: Jehoiakim, one of the last kings of Judah, taxed his people for money to pay off the king of _____.

4. TRUE OR TRICK: Nicodemus was a short, rich tax collector in Jericho.

5. TRUE OR TRICK: Even Jesus was taxed.

6. MULTIPLE CHOICE: What foreign king was warned by other subjects that the Jews would not pay taxes if he let them rebuild the city of Jerusalem?
  a. Artaxerxes
  b. Darius
  c. Belshazzar
  d. Nebuchadnezzar

7. TRUE OR TRICK: It was a tax collector who prayed, "God, I thank thee, that I am not as other men are."

8. QUOTE IT: Jesus replied, "Render to Caesar the things that are Caesar's, and to God the things that are God's" in response to the question, "Is it lawful. . ."

9. TRUE OR TRICK: When the Israelites returned to Jerusalem from Babylon, they had to borrow money to pay the king's tribute on their land.

10. TRUE OR TRICK: When the Israelites conquered Canaan, the Benjamites didn't drive out the people of the land but instead levied a tax on them.

Quiz 80
TEN COMMANDMENTS

The Ten Commandments are listed twice in the Old Testament—Exodus 20 and Deuteronomy 5. How much do you know about them?

1. TRUE OR TRICK: The commandment that Jesus said is the "first and great commandment" isn't actually on the table of the Ten Commandments.

2. QUOTE IT: Name as many of the first five commandments as you can.

3. QUOTE IT: Name as many of the last five commandments as you can.

4. MULTIPLE CHOICE: Only one commandment contains a promise, and that promise is
    a. you will prosper
    b. things will be well with you and you will live long
    c. you will inherit eternal life
    d. your children will call you blessed

5. MULTIPLE CHOICE: Who wrote the Ten Commandments on the first set of stone tablets that Moses brought down from Mount Sinai?

    a. God Himself

    b. Moses

    c. Joshua

    d. Bezaleel

6. FILL IN THE BLANK: Moses was on Mount Sinai, receiving the Ten Commandments, for _____ days and nights.

7. MULTIPLE CHOICE: Although God warned all the people to stay away from the mountain, one man was allowed to go up with Moses. That man was

    a. Aaron

    b. Joshua

    c. Caleb

    d. Eleazar

8. QUOTE IT: Before He gave Moses the Ten Commandments, God described Himself as "the LORD thy God, which have brought thee. . ."

9. FILL IN THE BLANK: God commanded His people not to work on the sabbath day because "in six days the LORD made heaven and earth, the sea, and all that in them is, and _____ the seventh day."

10. TRUE OR TRICK: "Love thy neighbour as thyself" is one of the Ten Commandments.

Quiz 81
THANK YOU! THANK YOU!

We can never thank God enough for all He's done for us, but an attitude of gratitude pleases Him. Are you as thankful as the people in this quiz?

1. MULTIPLE CHOICE: When Jesus healed ten lepers, only one returned to thank Him. The one who praised Jesus was a
    a. Pharisee
    b. Sadducee
    c. scribe
    d. Samaritan

2. MULTIPLE CHOICE: When Naaman was healed of his leprosy he praised
    a. God
    b. Elisha
    c. his Syrian gods
    d. a and b

3. FILL IN THE BLANK: The person who said, "My soul doth magnify the Lord and my spirit has rejoiced in God my savior" was _____.

4. TRUE OR TRICK: The apostle Paul urged Christians to give thanks in every good circumstance.

5. FILL IN THE BLANK: According to the Psalms, we are to enter the Lord's gates with _____ and into His courts with _____.

6. MULTIPLE CHOICE: To whom did Paul say, "I thank my God upon every remembrance of you"?
    a. Timothy
    b. Titus
    c. the Christians in Philippi
    d. the Christians in Rome

7. TRUE OR TRICK: In Nehemiah's day, there were priests in charge of thanksgiving.

8. QUOTE IT: The tax collector Zacchaeus joyfully climbed down from his perch in a tree when Jesus said, "Make haste, and come down; for today. . ."

9. MULTIPLE CHOICE: Who said, "I have learned, in whatsoever state I am, therewith to be content"?
    a. Peter
    b. Daniel
    c. Paul
    d. John

10. QUOTE IT: "O wretched man that I am! who shall deliver me from the body of this death? I thank God. . ."

Quiz 82
THEFT

Judas Iscariot condemned Mary for anointing Jesus' feet, saying the ointment should have been sold and the money given to the poor. But scripture says Judas didn't really care about the poor—he was a thief! What do you know about these other biblical thieves and thefts?

1. MULTIPLE CHOICE: After the battle of Jericho, who stole from the spoils of war even though God had strictly forbidden it?
    a. Zachariah
    b. Korah
    c. Achan
    d. Tola

2. TRUE OR TRICK: Because Elisha's servant, Gehazi, lied and stole from Naaman, Naaman's lameness was given to Gehazi and his seed forever.

3. TRUE OR TRICK: When Jacob left his father-in-law Laban to go back to his own country, Laban chased after Jacob and accused him of stealing his household gods.

4. FILL IN THE BLANK: In the prophecy of Malachi, God accused the priests of stealing from Him because they withheld their _____.

5. FILL IN THE BLANK: Jacob stole Esau's blessing from him with the help of _____.

6. QUOTE IT: When Jesus overthrew the moneychangers in the temple, He said, "It is written, My house shall be called the house of prayer; but Ye have. . ."

7. QUOTE IT: Just before Jesus said He had come to give His followers abundant life, He said that Satan, "the thief cometh not, but for to. . ."

8. MULTIPLE CHOICE: The Proverbs say that men do not despise a thief if he steals
    a. for someone else
    b. because he's hungry
    c. a rich man's goods
    d. from another thief

9. MULTIPLE CHOICE: Jesus said a thief and a robber would enter a sheepfold
    a. not by the door
    b. in disguise
    c. during the night hours
    d. all of the above

10. QUOTE IT: When a thief on a cross beside Jesus repented, the Lord told him, "Today shalt thou. . ."

Quiz 83
THE TRINITY

At Jesus' baptism, all three members of the Trinity were present in their distinct personages. The Father spoke from heaven and the Holy Spirit descended like a dove. How much do you know about this biblical mystery?

1. QUOTE IT: "And God said, Let us make man. . ."

2. FILL IN THE BLANK: In addition to Jesus' baptism, God the Father also said, "This is my beloved Son," on the occasion of Jesus' _____.

3. MULTIPLE CHOICE: When Jesus promised His disciples that He would send them the Holy Spirit after His ascension, He called the Spirit

    a. the Spirit of truth

    b. the Teacher

    c. the Comforter

    d. a and c

4. MULTIPLE CHOICE: When Jesus told the Jews, "I and my Father are one," the Jews

    a. believed Him

    b. wanted to stone Him

    c. worshipped Him

    d. tried to throw Him off a cliff

5. QUOTE IT: "In the beginning was the Word [Jesus], and the Word was with God, and. . ."

6. QUOTE IT: Jesus is described as being "the brightness of [God's] glory, and the. . ."

7. TRUE OR TRICK: In the beginning, the earth was without form and void and the spirit of God moved throughout the firmament.

8. FILL IN THE BLANK: Jesus told the disciples that after His Holy Spirit came on them they would be _____.

9. MULTIPLE CHOICE: Who said, "The grace of the Lord Jesus Christ, and the love of God, and the communion of the Holy Ghost, be with you all"?
    a. Paul
    b. James
    c. Jude
    d. Peter

10. FILL IN THE BLANKS: In Jesus' "Great Commission," He told His disciples to teach all nations and baptize them in the name of the _____, the _____, and the _____ _____.

Quiz 84
TROUBLOUS TIMES

From the moment Adam and Eve ate the forbidden fruit, this world has been full of trouble. What do you know about some of the biggest upheavals of Bible history?

1. MULTIPLE CHOICE: What king was told that because of his wickedness there would be no rain for three years?

    a. Rehoboam

    b. Manasseh

    c. Ahaziah

    d. Ahab

2. TRUE OR TRICK: Judah was already under bondage to the king of Egypt when Nebuchadnezzar attacked.

3. MULTIPLE CHOICE: Who was the last king of Israel when the Assyrians carried the nation into captivity?

    a. Solomon

    b. Hoshea

    c. Hezekiah

    d. Jehoiachin

4. FILL IN THE BLANK: Naomi, her husband, and their two sons left Bethlehem and went to Moab because there was a _____ in Judah.

5. QUOTE IT: Jesus said, "There shall be earthquakes in divers places, and there shall be famines and troubles. . ."

6. MULTIPLE CHOICE: How long did the plague on the Nile—the river turned to blood—last?
   a. twenty-four hours
   b. seven days
   c. a month
   d. two years

7. TRUE OR TRICK: When the king of Syria besieged Samaria, the famine was so severe that people were paying five pieces of silver for dove dung.

8. FILL IN THE BLANK: The Lord defended Hezekiah and Jerusalem by killing _____ Assyrian soldiers while they slept.

9. FILL IN THE BLANK: After Esther's intervention with the king of Persia, and the Jews were allowed to defend themselves against Haman's slaughter, the feast of _____ was instituted.

10. FILL IN THE BLANKS: When the fourth seal of Revelation was opened, a pale horse whose rider was named _____ appeared, and _____ followed him.

Quiz 85
TWELVE (OR SO) DISCIPLES

Jesus had twelve prominent disciples, but many beyond them—some of whom followed Him secretly. What do you know about these folks?

1. TRUE OR TRICK: Peter was a disciple of John the Baptist before he was a disciple of Jesus.

2. FILL IN THE BLANK: The name of the disciple chosen to take Judas Iscariot's place was _____.

3. TRUE OR TRICK: The wife of King Herod's steward was one woman who provided for Jesus' financial needs.

4. QUOTE IT: When a would-be disciple asked Jesus to let him go and bury his father, Jesus replied, "Follow me; and. . ."

5. MULTIPLE CHOICE: Which disciple brought the recently converted persecutor Saul to the apostles and vouched for him?
   a. Ananias
   b. Andrew
   c. Barnabas
   d. James

6. FILL IN THE BLANK: The number of male disciples at the crucifixion was _____. The number of female disciples at the crucifixion was _____.

7. QUOTE IT: "Joseph of Arimathaea, being a disciple of Jesus, but secretly. . ."

8. MULTIPLE CHOICE: When Jesus appointed disciples beyond His original twelve, sending them out two by two to "every city and place, whither he himself would come," how many were there?

    a. 24
    b. 36
    c. 70
    d. 120

9. FILL IN THE BLANK: The disciples were first called Christians in the city of _____.

10. TRUE OR TRICK: Paul considered himself to be the last of the apostles.

Quiz 86
THE "UN"-COLA

This quiz revolves around "un" words. How is your *un*derstanding?

1. FILL IN THE BLANK: "Be not forgetful to entertain strangers: for thereby some have entertained angels _____."

2. TRUE OR TRICK: When an ancient Israelite touched an unclean thing like a dead body, he was required to offer a burnt offering for his sin.

3. FILL IN THE BLANK: "The fear of the LORD is the beginning of wisdom: and the knowledge of the holy is _____."

4. QUOTE IT: The apostle Paul said that circumcision could become uncircumcision "if thou be..."

5. QUOTE IT: When Jesus told a frazzled father, "All things are possible to him that believeth," the man replied, "Lord, I believe..."

6. FILL IN THE BLANK: James said that visiting widows and the fatherless and keeping oneself unspotted by the world was pure and _____ religion.

7. MULTIPLE CHOICE: The apostle Paul told Timothy to keep the commandments so that Timothy's life would be

    a. unstained

    b. understandable

    c. unrebukable

    d. untouched by the world

8. MULTIPLE CHOICE: "Great is the LORD, and greatly to be praised; and his greatness is. . ."

    a. unfathomable

    b. unforgettable

    c. unknowable

    d. unsearchable

9. FILL IN THE BLANK: "A false witness shall not be _____, and he that speaketh lies shall not escape."

10. MULTIPLE CHOICE: We are to be merciful as God is merciful for He is kind to the

    a. unthankful

    b. unrighteous

    c. unbelievers

    d. unforgiving

Quiz 87
UP IN THE SKY

God said the lights of the firmament of heaven were to be for signs, seasons, days, and years (Genesis 1:14). What do you know about God's heavenly signs?

1. FILL IN THE BLANK: "The heavens declare the glory of God. . . . Day unto day uttereth speech, and night unto night sheweth _____."

2. TRUE OR TRICK: Jesus said that when the Son of Man comes in the clouds of heaven with power and great glory, all the tribes of the earth will see Him and mourn.

3. TRUE OR TRICK: Jesus noted that if the sky was red in the evening fair weather would follow, but if the sky was red in the morning there would be foul weather.

4. MULTIPLE CHOICE: The prophecy that a Star would come out of Jacob was made by
   a. Daniel
   b. Ezekiel
   c. Balaam
   d. Isaiah

5. MULTIPLE CHOICE: To whom was God speaking when He said, "Where wast thou when I laid the foundations of the earth. . . . when the morning stars sang together?"

    a. Moses

    b. Job

    c. Abraham

    d. Noah

6. FILL IN THE BLANK: The sun, moon, and stars were created on the _____ day of creation.

7. QUOTE IT: "Where is he that is born King of the Jews? for we have seen his star in the east, and. . ."

8. TRUE OR TRICK: When people worshipped Baal, they also worshipped the planets.

9. MULTIPLE CHOICE: When Hezekiah was sick and asked for a sign from God that God would heal him, God

    a. made the moon stand still

    b. made the sun stand still

    c. made the shadow on the sundial go backward

    d. made the planets align

10. QUOTE IT: God told Moses to stretch out his hand toward heaven, "that there may be darkness over the land of Egypt, even darkness. . ."

Quiz 88
VIGILANCE

The apostle Peter tells us to be sober and vigilant because our adversary the devil is like a roaring lion seeking to devour us. What do you know about these examples of vigilance (or lack thereof) in scripture?

1. MULTIPLE CHOICE: The orphaned Esther was looked after carefully by Mordecai, who was her
- a. family friend
- b. uncle
- c. cousin
- d. grandfather

2. FILL IN THE BLANK: When five foolish virgins in a parable of Jesus didn't bring enough oil for their lamps, they couldn't keep watch for the _____.

3. QUOTE IT: When angels appeared to shepherds outside Bethlehem, the shepherds were "abiding in the field. . ."

4. MULTIPLE CHOICE: "Therefore let us not sleep, as do others; but let us watch and. . ."
- a. love
- b. keep the faith
- c. be sober
- d. forgive

5. TRUE OR TRICK: When King Saul sent men to young David's house to watch him through the night and kill him in the morning, Saul's daughter Michal helped him to escape.

6. QUOTE IT: "Be ye stedfast, unmoveable, always abounding in the work of the Lord, forasmuch as ye know. . ."

7. MULTIPLE CHOICE: "Let us not be weary in well doing; for in due season we shall reap, if we. . ."
    a. faint not
    b. run with patience the race set before us
    c. look unto Jesus the author and finisher of our faith
    d. love one another

8. MULTIPLE CHOICE: Which church leader, according to the apostle Paul, should be "vigilant, sober, of good behaviour, given to hospitality, apt to teach"?
    a. pastor
    b. evangelist
    c. bishop
    d. deacon

9. QUOTE IT: God warned Cain about his attitude toward his brother, Abel, saying, "If thou doest well, shalt thou not be accepted? And if thou doest not well. . ."

10. FILL IN THE BLANKS: "If I take the wings of the morning, and dwell in the uttermost parts of the sea; even there shall thy hand _____ me, and thy right hand shall _____ me."

Quiz 89
VILLAINS AND TROUBLEMAKERS

Perhaps the most notorious villain in the Bible is Judas Iscariot. . .but what do you know about these other troublemakers?

1. FILL IN THE BLANK: The villain associated with the story of Esther is "this wicked _____."

2. FILL IN THE BLANKS: Israel's most evil king and queen, in the eyes of the Lord, were _____ and _____.

3. MULTIPLE CHOICE: When Korah and his rebels tried to usurp Moses' authority, the Lord made their punishment a "new thing." That "new thing" was that
    a. they were consumed by fire
    b. a mountain fell on them
    c. the earth opened up and swallowed them
    d. they vanished into thin air

4. TRUE OR TRICK: Og, the king of Bashan who fought the Israelites, was a giant.

5. MULTIPLE CHOICE: Which one of Jacob's sons made the suggestion to throw their young brother Joseph into a pit?

    a. Gad

    b. Levi

    c. Simeon

    d. Reuben

6. MULTIPLE CHOICE: Which of Joseph's brothers made the suggestion to sell Joseph to slavers?

    a. Reuben

    b. Dan

    c. Judah

    d. Issachar

7. TRUE OR TRICK: The magicians and wise men of Babylon tricked King Darius into signing a decree that put Daniel in the lions' den.

8. MULTIPLE CHOICE: Jannes and Jambres were

    a. deserters from Gideon's army

    b. the soldiers who killed King Zimri

    c. Egyptian magicians who stood against Moses

    d. Jews who tried to kill Paul

9. TRUE OR TRICK: The name *Antichrist* is mentioned in 1 and 2 John but not in Revelation.

10. QUOTE IT: "Certain of the Jews banded together, and bound themselves under a curse, saying that they would neither eat nor drink till. . ."

Quiz 90
THE VIRGIN BIRTH

There are a lot of Christmas traditions around the world...
but what do you know about the biblical account of God's
greatest gift of love?

1. FILL IN THE BLANK: When Matthew wrote "behold a
virgin shall conceive," he was quoting the prophet _____.

2. MULTIPLE CHOICE: When the wise men asked Herod,
"Where is he that is born King of the Jews?" (Matthew 2:2),
the chief priests and scribes knew He was in Bethlehem,
as foretold by the prophet
    a. Hosea
    b. Zechariah
    c. Micah
    d. Joel

3. QUOTE IT: "Then Herod, when he saw that he was
mocked of the wise men...slew all the children that were
in Bethlehem, and in all the coasts thereof, from..."

4. TRUE OR TRICK: The shepherds that the angels
appeared to were on the outskirts of Bethlehem.

5. FILL IN THE BLANK: Jesus was presented at the
temple when He was _____ days old.

6. MULTIPLE CHOICE: The sacrifice that Joseph and Mary gave for Jesus to the Lord was

    a. a lamb

    b. a ram

    c. two turtledoves

    d. a goat

7. TRUE OR TRICK: God told Joseph to take Mary and Jesus to Nazareth to keep them safe from Herod.

8. QUOTE IT: An angel told the shepherds, "And this shall be a sign unto you. . ."

9. MULTIPLE CHOICE: Joseph and Mary had traveled from Nazareth to Bethlehem because

    a. they knew Jesus had to be born in Bethlehem

    b. Elizabeth and Zechariah had their son in Bethlehem

    c. God told Joseph in a dream to go to Bethlehem

    d. all the world was being taxed

10. QUOTE IT: "She brought forth her firstborn son. . . and laid him in a manger; because. . ."

Quiz 91
WARS AND RUMORS OF WARS

Jesus said that wars and rumors of wars would be a sign of the end times. But there were also wars and rumors of wars all through the Bible. What do you know about these?

1. MULTIPLE CHOICE: The first war mentioned in the Bible directly affected

    a. Noah

    b. Lot

    c. Jacob

    d. b and c

2. TRUE OR TRICK: The last war mentioned in the Bible has Jesus as commander.

3. MULTIPLE CHOICE: Gideon's army of three hundred men fought against the army of the Midianites, who were descendants of

    a. Moses

    b. Abraham

    c. Lot

    d. Aaron

4. TRUE OR TRICK: One of God's rules for war was that His people should not cut down any trees when besieging a city.

5. FILL IN THE BLANK: When Saul was king, he warred against the _____ more than any other people.

6. FILL IN THE BLANK: Jeremiah prophesied about _____ the king of _____ making war against God's people.

7. TRUE OR TRICK: The Bible says the Lord despises war.

8. QUOTE IT: When Israel divided, with Solomon's son Rehoboam as king in the south and Jeroboam as king in the north, "there was war between Rehoboam and Jeroboam..."

9. MULTIPLE CHOICE: Which of the following is *not* among Moses' acceptable excuses for leaving military service?

    a. soldier has just built a house but has not yet lived in it
    b. soldier is engaged to a woman but not yet married
    c. soldier is fainthearted or afraid
    d. soldier has large herds of livestock to oversee

10. QUOTE IT: "Nation shall not lift up a sword against nation, neither shall they..."

Quiz 92
WATER LINES

Water is extremely important, for many reasons. Do you know what the Bible has to say about this vital substance?

1. TRUE OR TRICK: Jesus told Mary and Martha that He was the living water.

2. FILL IN THE BLANK: God used a flood to defeat the Moabites on behalf of King Jehoshaphat in the days of the prophet _____.

3. QUOTE IT: "Cast thy bread upon the waters: for thou shalt find it. . ."

4. FILL IN THE BLANKS: "I will pour water upon him that is _____, and floods upon the dry _____."

5. TRUE OR TRICK: The Bible says that God sends rain on the just and the unjust.

6. QUOTE IT: God told Solomon that if He shut up the heavens and stopped the rain, He would also heal the land if His people would "humble themselves, and pray. . ."

7. MULTIPLE CHOICE: Who was the only person to cross the Jordan River on dry land twice?

    a. Joshua
    b. Moses
    c. Elijah
    d. Elisha

8. TRUE OR TRICK: When God parted the waters of the Red Sea, the Israelites passed through on dry land.

9. FILL IN THE BLANK: John the Baptist said he baptized with water unto _____.

10. FILL IN THE BLANK: In the book of Revelation, John saw a new heaven and new earth but there was no more _____.

Quiz 93
WISDOM AND FOLLY

Proverbs 9:10 says, "The fear of the LORD is the beginning of wisdom." Many are wise—but many are foolish. What do you know about both?

1. TRUE OR TRICK: The Bible says both to answer a fool according to his folly and not to answer a fool according to his folly.

2. QUOTE IT: The foolish man "built his house upon the sand: and the rain descended, and the floods came, and the winds blew, and beat upon that house; and it fell. . ."

3. QUOTE IT: "Teach us to number our days, that we may. . ."

4. TRUE OR TRICK: In Jesus' parable of the rich fool, the man said to himself, "Eat, drink, and be merry."

5. MULTIPLE CHOICE: The book of Ecclesiastes says that wisdom is better than
   a. food
   b. drink
   c. love
   d. weapons of war

6. MULTIPLE CHOICE: To whom did God say, "Does the hawk fly by thy wisdom?"

    a. Isaiah

    b. Elijah

    c. Job

    d. Jonah

7. FILL IN THE BLANK: Solomon was considered to be the wisest man on earth but when he was old his heart was turned to other gods by his _____.

8. MULTIPLE CHOICE: The wisdom that is from above is

    a. pure and peaceable

    b. gentle

    c. full of mercy

    d. all of the above

9. QUOTE IT: "If any of you lack wisdom, let him ask of God. . ."

10. QUOTE IT: "The fool hath said in his heart. . .

Quiz 94
WOMEN FOLK

The Bible is filled with amazing women who did amazing things. How much do you know about these?

1. TRUE OR TRICK: Zipporah circumcised her son after God threatened to kill her husband, Moses.

2. FILL IN THE BLANK: The apostles chose seven men to administer the daily portions among the widows because the _____ widows were being neglected.

3. MULTIPLE CHOICE: The only two women mentioned by name in the Hebrews 11 list of the faithful are
    a. Eve and Sarah
    b. Ruth and Naomi
    c. Esther and Rahab
    d. Rahab and Sarah

4. TRUE OR TRICK: Bathsheba is mentioned in the genealogy of Jesus in Matthew 1.

5. MULTIPLE CHOICE: Candace was the queen of
    a. Egypt
    b. Sheba
    c. Ethiopia
    d. Israel

6. TRUE OR TRICK: The five daughters of a man named Zebadiah got the laws of ancient Israel changed to allow women the right to inherit land as men always had.

7. MULTIPLE CHOICE: Jael was a woman who
    a. was a slave of King Saul
    b. watered all of Abraham's camels
    c. drove a tent peg through the head of an enemy commander
    d. was one of David's wives

8. FILL IN THE BLANK: The woman of Shunem is associated with the prophet _____.

9. TRUE OR TRICK: In the book of Revelation, the "whore of Babylon" pursues a pregnant woman into the wilderness to destroy her unborn baby.

10. MULTIPLE CHOICE: Sarah's handmaid Hagar was
    a. a Moabite
    b. an Israelite
    c. an Egyptian
    d. an Amalekite

Quiz 95
X MARKS THE SPOT

The Bible is full of treasures, both spiritual and material. What do you recall about these?

1. QUOTE IT: When a merchant "had found one pearl of great price, [he] went and. . ."

2. MULTIPLE CHOICE: God set ambushes against the Ammonites and Moabites when King Jehoshaphat and his people prayed—they didn't even have to fight. How many days did it take for God's people to carry away the spoil?

    a. one
    b. two
    c. three
    d. seven

3. FILL IN THE BLANK: When Jacob left his father-in-law, Laban chased after his son-in-law because someone (later determined to be Laban's daughter Rachel) had stolen his _____.

4. QUOTE IT: Jesus said, "Where your treasure is. . ."

5. FILL IN THE BLANK: In heaven, twenty-four elders cast their _____ before God's throne.

6. MULTIPLE CHOICE: The Jewish king who paid a tax to the king of Assyria with the silver and gold from the temple was

  a. Ahab

  b. Jehoshaphat

  c. Uzziah

  d. Hezekiah

7. MULTIPLE CHOICE: What, according to Moses, comes out of God's "good treasure"?

  a. salvation

  b. rain

  c. gold

  d. peace

8. QUOTE IT: "Better is little with the fear of the LORD than great treasure and. . ."

9. MULTIPLE CHOICE: What did Moses consider "greater riches than the treasures in Egypt"?

  a. the reproach of Christ

  b. the pleasure of God

  c. the joy of service

  d. the hope of heaven

10. FILL IN THE BLANK: The wise men brought Jesus treasures of _____, _____, and _____.

Quiz 96
YEARNINGS

Though the apostle Paul yearned to preach to the Jews, God sent him to the Gentiles. What do you know about these other biblical yearnings?

1. QUOTE IT: "Seek ye first the kingdom of God, and his righteousness; and. . ."

2. TRUE OR TRICK: The Queen of Sheba visited Solomon to ask him hard questions about the Lord.

3. FILL IN THE BLANKS: The rich young ruler who approached Jesus yearned for _____ _____.

4. TRUE OR TRICK: Abraham longed for a proper wife for his son Isaac, so he sent a servant to their distant relatives to find one.

5. FILL IN THE BLANK: God sent Paul a vision of a man saying, "Come over into _____ and help us."

6. FILL IN THE BLANK: Jacob served a total of _____ years to earn the right to marry his beloved Rachel.

7. MULTIPLE CHOICE: The laws of the Lord are more to be desired than
    a. silver
    b. life
    c. rubies
    d. gold

8. FILL IN THE BLANK: The Messiah is described as "the desire of all _____."

9. MULTIPLE CHOICE: Which of his eleven brothers did Joseph, as second-in-command of Egypt, yearn for?
    a. Reuben
    b. Gad
    c. Simeon
    d. Benjamin

10. TRUE OR TRICK: David said that one thing he desired of God was to dwell in the house of the Lord all the days of his life.

Quiz 97
YOUTH GROUP

Growing up can be fun, exciting, or scary—and sometimes all of those things at once. It was no different in Bible times. What do you know about scripture's "youth group"?

1. FILL IN THE BLANK: When Mary and Joseph found young Jesus in the temple astonishing the elders with His wisdom, Jesus was _____ years old.

2. QUOTE IT: When Jesus was going to feed the five thousand, Andrew brought him a small boy, "a lad here, which hath. . ."

3. MULTIPLE CHOICE: When David was a youth, he tended his father's
  a. cattle
  b. crops
  c. sheep
  d. a and c

4. QUOTE IT: When Pharaoh's daughter rescued a baby from the Nile River, she named him Moses, "and she said, Because. . ."

5. MULTIPLE CHOICE: The person who told the Syrian army commander Naaman the leper about Elisha the prophet was

    a. his boy slave

    b. his son

    c. his wife's maid

    d. his wife's nephew

6. FILL IN THE BLANK: When Abraham took his son to the mountains of Moriah, Isaac said to his father, "Behold the fire and the wood: but where is the _____ for a burnt offering?"

7. MULTIPLE CHOICE: The young boy who heard God's voice at nighttime was

    a. Solomon

    b. Eli

    c. Samuel

    d. David

8. QUOTE IT: The Proverbs say, "Train up a child in the way he should go: and when he is old. . ."

9. TRUE OR TRICK: Paul once preached so long that a young man fell asleep, dropped out a window, and died.

10. TRUE OR TRICK: Jacob's youngest son was originally named Benoni by his mother, Leah.

Quiz 98
"Z" PEOPLE

As the title suggests, this quiz is about people whose names start with Z. How many are familiar to you?

1. TRUE OR TRICK: In the order of Bible books, the prophet Zechariah comes before the prophet Zephaniah.

2. MULTIPLE CHOICE: Zebulun was one of the twelve sons of Jacob. His mother was
    a. Leah
    b. Rachel
    c. Bilhah
    d. Zilpah

3. TRUE OR TRICK: Zilpah was Leah's handmaiden.

4. FILL IN THE BLANK: Zadok was a priest during the reign of King _____.

5. MULTIPLE CHOICE: Who was the famous (or infamous) husband of Zeresh?
    a. Judas Iscariot
    b. Haman
    c. King Omri
    d. Balaam

6. FILL IN THE BLANK: Zebedee was the father of two of Jesus' disciples: _____ and _____.

7. TRUE OR TRICK: Zedekiah was the last king of Israel.

8. FILL IN THE BLANK: Zerubbabel was _____ of Judah in the days of Haggai the prophet.

9. MULTIPLE CHOICE: Zimran was the son of
  a. Abraham
  b. Moses
  c. Joshua
  d. Caleb

10. MULTIPLE CHOICE: Zimri, one of the evil kings of Israel, had a reign lasting only
  a. a day
  b. a week
  c. a month
  d. a year

Quiz 99
ZACCHAEUS THE CONVERT

A children's song says, "Zacchaeus was a wee little man." Other than his diminutive stature, what do you know about him?

1. FILL IN THE BLANK: Zacchaeus's story is only found in the gospel of _____.

2. MULTIPLE CHOICE: Zacchaeus was the chief
    a. leader in the Temple
    b. priest
    c. leader of the Sanhedrin
    d. tax collector

3. FILL IN THE BLANK: Zacchaeus climbed a _____ tree in order to see Jesus.

4. QUOTE IT: When He saw the little man up in the tree, Jesus said, "Zacchaeus. . ."

5. FILL IN THE BLANK: The crowd murmured about Jesus because they considered Zacchaeus a _____.

6. MULTIPLE CHOICE: Zacchaeus came down and received Jesus

    a. humbly

    b. quietly

    c. joyfully

    d. reverently

7. MULTIPLE CHOICE: When Zacchaeus saw the Lord, Jesus was passing through

    a. Jerusalem

    b. Jericho

    c. Nazareth

    d. Galilee

8. QUOTE IT: Jesus told Zacchaeus, "The Son of Man is come to seek and. . ."

9. MULTIPLE CHOICE: Zacchaeus told Jesus that he would restore anything he had taken from anyone by false accusation

    a. to the exact amount

    b. double

    c. triple

    d. fourfold

10. TRUE OR TRICK: Jesus told Zacchaeus, "To day I must abide at thy house."

Quiz 100
ZEALOUS OF GOOD WORKS

Zeal is defined as passionate dedication. What do you recall about these zealous biblical people?

1. MULTIPLE CHOICE: What descendant of Aaron was given a "covenant of an everlasting priesthood" because he made atonement for the children of Israel?

    a. Eleazar

    b. Abihu

    c. Phinehas

    d. Nadab

2. TRUE OR TRICK: The king who slew Ahab and all his house claimed to be filled with the zeal of the Lord.

3. TRUE OR TRICK: Jesus said, "The zeal of thine house hath eaten me up."

4. MULTIPLE CHOICE: About what did Isaiah say, "The zeal of the LORD of hosts will perform this"?

    a. the unending kingdom of God

    b. the salvation of Israel

    c. triumph over the Antichrist

    d. the salvation of the Gentiles

5. TRUE OR TRICK: One of Jesus' twelve disciples was called Simon the Zealot.

6. QUOTE IT: The apostle Paul said the people of Israel "have a zeal of God, but not. . ."

7. MULTIPLE CHOICE: Paul described one person as having a great zeal for the Christians at Colosse. That person was
    a. Onesimus
    b. Philemon
    c. Epaphras
    d. Paul himself

8. TRUE OR TRICK: When Hezekiah purged idolatrous worship from Judah, he broke up the brass snake that Moses had made in the wilderness because people were burning incense to it.

9. MULTIPLE CHOICE: Which of the seven churches of Asia Minor was urged by Jesus to be zealous?
    a. Philadelphia
    b. Ephesus
    c. Thyatira
    d. Laodicea

10. QUOTE IT: "It is good to be zealously affected always. . ."

ANSWERS

QUIZ 1: "A" PEOPLE

1. d (Joshua 7:21)
2. Trick. She was David's wife (1 Samuel 25:39)
3. "taken up between the heaven and the earth" (2 Samuel 18:9)
4. c (Daniel 1:7)
5. True (1 Kings 15:11)
6. Trick. He was captain of Saul's army (1 Samuel 14:50)
7. True (Luke 3:2)
8. d (Luke 2:36–38)
9. a (Acts 21:10)
10. "above all that were before him" (1 Kings 16:30)

QUIZ 2: ABUNDANCE

1. "follow me all the days of my life" (Psalm 23:6)
2. "running over" (Luke 6:38)
3. a (Proverbs 10:22)
4. "for they shall inherit the earth" (Matthew 5:5)
5. given, find, opened (Matthew 7:7)
6. b (Genesis 1:21–22)
7. c (2 Chronicles 17:4–5)
8. life (Revelation 2:7)
9. Trick. "Blessings are upon the *head* of the just" (Proverbs 10:6)
10. c (Ephesians 1:3)

QUIZ 3: ALL CREATURES, GREAT AND SMALL

1. Trick. Adam named the animals (Genesis 2:19)
2. bear, lion (1 Samuel 17:34–36)
3. d (a: Genesis 8; b: Matthew 3:16; c: The name Jonah means "dove")
4. "for a rich man to enter into the kingdom of God" (Matthew 19:24)
5. b (Numbers 22:30 NIV)
6. d (Leviticus 11:4)
7. "and without spot" (1 Peter 1:19)
8. True (Exodus 8:7)
9. True, in the King James Version. The New International Version calls them "wild oxen" (Psalm 92:10)
10. lion (Proverbs 30:30)

QUIZ 4: ANGELS AMONG US

1. True (Isaiah 6:2)
2. "one of the chief princes" (Daniel 10:13)
3. c (Michael, Revelation 12:7; Gabriel, Luke 1:26; Lucifer,

Isaiah 14:12; Abaddon, Revelation 9:11)

4. True (Psalm 78:24–25)

5. d (2 Corinthians 11:14)

6. b (a: Genesis 32:1–2; c: Luke 2:8, 13; d: 2 Kings 6:14, 17)

7. "that there should be time no longer" (Revelation 10:6)

8. Cornelius (Acts 10:3)

9. d (Psalm 91:11–12)

10. Saints, or Christians (1 Corinthians 6:3)

QUIZ 5: BABIES BORN

1. "are in thy womb" (Genesis 25:22–23)

2. Isaac's (Genesis 21:5–6)

3. a (Isaiah 8:1)

4. Samuel (1 Samuel 1:20–28)

5. True (Luke 1:11–13)

6. Trick. Moses was from the tribe of Levi (Exodus 2:1–10)

7. c (Hosea 1:2–11)

8. Trick. The angel told Samson's mother (Judges 13:3–5)

9. d (Ruth 4:17)

10. Trick. Elisha raised the woman's son from the dead
    (2 Kings 4:32–36)

QUIZ 6: BORN AGAIN

1. Damascus (Acts 9:2–3)

2. "regeneration" (Titus 3:5)

3. "what must I do to be saved?" (Acts 16:30)

4. a (Acts 8:36–38)

5. "into his mother's womb, and be born?" (John 3:4)

6. True (Acts 10:25, 44–45)

7. Trick. Agrippa said that he was "almost" persuaded (Acts 26:28)

8. d (Acts 16:14)

9. c (Acts 2:41)

10. c (Acts 8:18–20)

QUIZ 7: BROTHERLY LOVE

1. continue (Hebrews 13:1)

2. c (Judges 3:9)

3. Trick. Aaron was Moses' older brother (Exodus 7:7)

4. charity, or love (2 Peter 1:7)

5. beareth, believeth, hopeth, endureth (1 Corinthians 13:7)

6. a (Genesis 11:31)

7. adversity (Proverbs 17:17)

8. True (John 1:40–42)

9. "meant it unto good" (Genesis 50:20)
10. Trick. Jonathan was David's nephew (2 Samuel 21:21)

QUIZ 8: CHARITY CASES
1. b (Acts 9:39)
2. Trick. He had an infirmity for thirty-eight years (John 5:5)
3. c (1 Kings 17:13–14)
4. beggar (Mark 10:46)
5. True (2 Kings 25:27–30)
6. "let him first cast a stone at her" (John 8:7)
7. Mephibosheth (2 Samuel 9:1–7)
8. d (John 4:7)
9. "In the name of Jesus Christ of Nazareth rise up and walk" (Acts 3:6)
10. b (Ruth 2:1–5)

QUIZ 9: COURAGE, MAN, COURAGE!
1. "been with Jesus" (Acts 4:13)
2. c (Joshua 1:1–6)
3. Trick (though all of those characteristics together likely provide courage)
4. "boldly" (Hebrews 4:16)
5. d (Mark 15:43)
6. "he shall strengthen thine/your heart" (Psalm 27:14, 31:24)
7. a (Judges 6–7)
8. Trick. Paul wrote that to Timothy (2 Timothy 1:7).
9. "perfect love" (1 John 4:18)
10. b (1 Samuel 17:50)

QUIZ 10: COWS AND OTHER LIVESTOCK
1. c (Psalm 50:10)
2. True (Genesis 13:5–9)
3. ninety-nine (Matthew 18:12)
4. b (Malachi 1:6–8)
5. "we have turned every one to his own way" (Isaiah 53:6)
6. swine, or pigs (Luke 15:15)
7. True (Genesis 30:32)
8. ram (Genesis 22:13)
9. True. Jair had thirty (Judges 10:3–4); Abdon had seventy (Judges 12:13–14)
10. b (Deuteronomy 17:16)

QUIZ 11: THE CRUCIFIXION
1. Trick. It was John who witnessed the crucifixion (John 19:26)

2. b (Matthew 27:32)
3. three (John 19:19–20)
4. "I have written" (John 19:21–22)
5. "Father, forgive them" (Luke 23:34)
6. a (John 19:24)
7. "shalt thou be with me in paradise" (Luke 23:43)
8. Trick. It tore from top to bottom (Matthew 27:51)
9. three (Luke 23:44)
10. True (Matthew 27:52)

QUIZ 12: DARING DANIEL
1. Belteshazzar (Daniel 1:7)
2. Trick. He interpreted a dream for King Nebuchadnezzar (Daniel 4:18)
3. c (Daniel 1:15)
4. three (Daniel 6:10)
5. True (Daniel 1:3–4)
6. knowledge, wisdom (Daniel 1:17)
7. "would not defile himself" (Daniel 1:8)
8. Trick. The hand wrote a message to Belshazzar (Daniel 5)
9. Trick. Gabriel appeared to Daniel (Daniel 8:16)
10. d (Daniel 12:9)

QUIZ 13: DAVID, THE MAN AFTER GOD'S OWN HEART
1. c (Acts 13:16, 22)
2. True (Ruth 4:21–22)
3. Judah (Matthew 1:3–6)
4. "but the Lord looketh on the heart" (1 Samuel 16:7)
5. True (1 Chronicles 23–26)
6. c (1 Chronicles 15:29)
7. musical instruments (2 Chronicles 7:6)
8. "Thou art the man" (2 Samuel 12:7)
9. Trick. They did eat the bread (1 Samuel 21:6)
10. True (1 Samuel 27:7)

QUIZ 14: DAYS OF CREATION
1. the heaven and the earth (Genesis 1:1)
2. "and there was light" (Genesis 1:3)
3. True (Genesis 1:5, 8)
4. grass, herbs, and trees (Genesis 1:12)
5. c (Genesis 1:16–19)
6. kind, kind (Genesis 1:25)
7. d (Genesis 1:14)

8. True (Genesis 1:21)

9. "in our image" (Genesis 1:26)

10. woman (Genesis 2:22)

QUIZ 15: DEVIL AND DEMONS

1. "and tremble" (James 2:19)

2. True (Matthew 12:24)

3. "prayer and fasting" (Matthew 17:21)

4. b (Luke 8:2)

5. salvation, righteousness, faith (Ephesians 6:11–17)

6. Trick (Matthew 8:28–29)

7. c (Acts 19:11–12)

8. True (Job 1:6)

9. b (Luke 10:18)

10. "the Lord thy God" (Matthew 4:7)

QUIZ 16: DREAMS AND DREAMERS

1. c (Matthew 1:20; 2:13; 2:19)

2. butler, baker (Genesis 40)

3. Trick. It was Pilate's wife who dreamed about Jesus (Matthew 27:19). Fun fact: this is the only biblical record of a woman having a dream—and she was a Gentile!

4. "I knew it not" (Genesis 28:16)

5. b (Acts 10:9–16)

6. True (Judges 7:11–14)

7. c (Acts 2:16)

8. "Ask what I shall give thee" (1 Kings 3:5)

9. a (1 Samuel 28:6)

10. True (Job 7:14)

QUIZ 17: EARTHQUAKES AND OTHER DISASTERS

1. d. Earthquakes occurred in the stories of Elijah (1 Kings 19:11–13), Paul and Silas (Acts 16:25–26), and Jesus (Matthew 27:50–51)

2. forty, forty (Genesis 7:12)

3. b (Numbers 16:28–32)

4. Trick. It hailed on the Amorites (Joshua 10:6–11)

5. c (1 Kings 17:1)

6. famine (Genesis 41:27)

7. "Peace, be still" (Mark 4:39)

8. "the wrath of the Lamb" (Revelation 6:16)

9. Trick. They moved due to a famine (Ruth 1:1)

10. c (Exodus 8:6–7)

QUIZ 18: EMMANUEL

1. "he shall save his people from their sins" (Matthew 1:21)
2. Lion (Revelation 5:5)
3. c (Mark 11:29–30)
4. True (Luke 7:20)
5. c (Luke 3:23)
6. True (Matthew 16:14)
7. "the Christ, the Son of the living God" (Matthew 16:16)
8. "Render therefore unto Caesar the things which are Caesar's; and unto God the things that are God's" (Matthew 22:17–21)
9. "take up thy bed, and go thy way" (Mark 2:11)
10. d (Mark 2:23–28)

QUIZ 19: EXCELLENT ESTHER

1. True
2. c (Esther 2:7)
3. cousin (Esther 2:7)
4. Benjamin (Esther 2:5)
5. c (Esther 3:5–6)
6. "the banquet that I have prepared for him" (Esther 5:4)
7. True (Esther 6:6, 10)
8. Vashti (Esther 1:15)
9. b (Esther 1:3)
10. True (Esther 8:11)

QUIZ 20: FALSE GODS

1. "no other gods before me" (Exodus 20:2–3)
2. True (1 Samuel 5:1–5)
3. d (Acts 19:24–28)
4. a (2 Kings 18:1, 4)
5. Jezebel (1 Kings 16:31–32)
6. Trick. But Zeus (or Jupiter) is, in Acts 14:12.
7. c (1 Kings 11:7)
8. True. King Jeroboam made two golden calves (1 Kings 12:26–28)
9. d (2 Kings 23:13–14)
10. meat (1 Corinthians 10:28)

QUIZ 21: FEAR NOT

1. love (1 John 4:18)
2. c (Joshua 1:9)
3. "of a sound mind" (2 Timothy 1:7)
4. Trick (Matthew 10:28)

5. d (Matthew 28:1–5)

6. Trick. They stayed in the wilderness (Genesis 21:17–21)

7. "the right hand of my righteousness" (Isaiah 41:10)

8. d (Genesis 50:19)

9. reward (Genesis 15:1)

10. "It is I" (Matthew 14:27)

QUIZ 22: FIRE!

1. "Son of God" (Daniel 3:25)

2. "the devil and his angels" (Matthew 25:41)

3. c (2 Kings 1:10)

4. True (Exodus 9:23)

5. brimstone (Genesis 19:24)

6. Samson (Judges 15:4–5)

7. True (Matthew 3:11)

8. Pentecost (Acts 2:1–3)

9. d (Amos 4:11–12)

10. "their worm dieth not" (Mark 9:47–48)

QUIZ 23: FOUR-SYLLABLE NAMES

1. b (Exodus 6:23)

2. Jeremiah (Jeremiah 26:18–19)

3. "blessed is the fruit of thy womb" (Luke 1:42)

4. a (Ruth 1:2)

5. Philemon

6. "nine hundred sixty and nine years" (Genesis 5:27)

7. True (Mark 10:46–52)

8. True (Genesis 14:18)

9. a (1 Kings 11:43)

10. Trick. His name was Lazarus (Luke 16:22–23)

QUIZ 24: GENEALOGIES

1. Seth (Genesis 4:25)

2. Trick (Genesis 25:28)

3. Shem, Ham, and Japheth (Genesis 5:32)

4. Trick. The news that the ark had been taken is what killed him (1 Samuel 4:17–18)

5. Leah, Rachel (Genesis 29:16)

6. c (Genesis 34:1)

7. d. Gideon was also called Jerubbaal (Judges 6:32; 9:1–6)

8. a. His sons were named Gershom and Eliezer (Exodus 18:2–4)

9. Joseph, Benjamin (Genesis 30:24; 35:18)

10. True (2 Samuel 13)

QUIZ 25: GETTING FROM HERE TO THERE

1. "that bringeth good tidings" (Isaiah 52:7)
2. c (Exodus 15:21)
3. d (Numbers 22)
4. iron (Judges 4:13)
5. True (2 Kings 9:20)
6. c (John 6)
7. Trick. On the seventh day they walked around seven times (Joshua 6:4)
8. True (1 Kings 18:46)
9. d (1 Samuel 17:17)
10. Trick. The Bible doesn't say how Nebuchadnezzar got Jehoiakim to Babylon (2 Chronicles 36:6)

QUIZ 26: GIFTED

1. True (Judges 16:20)
2. harp (1 Samuel 16:23)
3. Spirit, Lord, God (1 Corinthians 12:4–6)
4. a (Exodus 4:10–16)
5. "a double portion of thy spirit be upon me" (2 Kings 2:9)
6. b (2 Timothy 1:6)
7. True (1 Samuel 10:10–11)
8. the Gentiles (Acts 26:16–17)
9. Jonah (Jonah 1:3)
10. True (Ephesians 4:11–12)

QUIZ 27: THE GOLDEN RULE

1. d (Matthew 7:12; Luke 6:31)
2. True (Matthew 5–7)
3. "do ye even so to them" (Matthew 7:12)
4. c (Luke 10:25–37)
5. Trick. Jesus told him to sell all he had and give it to the poor (Luke 18:22)
6. c (Matthew 5:1)
7. a (Matthew 7:11)
8. "asketh of thee" (Luke 6:30)
9. law, prophets (Matthew 7:12)
10. Trick

QUIZ 28: HEAVEN ABOVE

1. life (Genesis 3:22; Revelation 22:2)
2. "as the angels of God in heaven" (Matthew 22:30)
3. treasures (Matthew 6:20)

4. Trick. Paul says "a man" (2 Corinthians 12:2)
5. silence (Revelation 8:1)
6. "were passed away" (Revelation 21:1)
7. "right hand" (Hebrews 12:2)
8. True (Revelation 4:3)
9. Trick. Jesus was standing there (Acts 7:55–56)
10. d (Revelation 4:4)

QUIZ 29: HI, PRIESTS

1. Melchizedek (Genesis 14:18)
2. True (Numbers 35:25)
3. True. The high priests were Annas and Caiaphas (Luke 3:2)
4. "Holiness to the Lord" (Exodus 28:36)
5. God (Exodus 28:1)
6. Sadducees (Acts 5:17)
7. c (Exodus 32:26–29)
8. b (Malachi 1:6)
9. True (Luke 1:5)
10. True (Acts 23:1–5)

QUIZ 30: HOLY, HOLY, HOLY

1. "Thou God seest me" (Genesis 16:13)
2. c (Exodus 20:2)
3. Jehovahjireh (Genesis 22:14)
4. Trick. He describes a "perfect law of liberty" (James 1:25)
5. c (Psalm 132:2 calls Him the "mighty God of Jacob")
6. "the sons [or children] of God" (1 John 3:1)
7. c (Romans 8:28)
8. good, everlasting, endureth (Psalm 100:5)
9. Trick. God knows us from our mother's womb (verse 13).
10. righteousness, uprightness (Psalm 9:8)

QUIZ 31: THE HUMAN BODY

1. "wonderfully made" (Psalm 139:14)
2. dust, dust (Genesis 3:19)
3. True (1 Samuel 10:23)
4. True (Exodus 17:9–11)
5. c (Judges 16:7)
6. hand (Isaiah 59:1)
7. "blessing and cursing" (James 3:10)
8. Trick. It is the tongue (James 3:8)
9. c (Proverbs 6:10–11)
10. Ezekiel (Ezekiel 37:4–10)

QUIZ 32: HUSBANDS AND WIVES

1. "bear rule in his own house" (Esther 1:22)
2. Trick. "He had seven hundred wives, princesses, and three hundred concubines" (1 Kings 11:3)
3. b (Genesis 26:34–35)
4. "put her away privily" (Matthew 1:18–19)
5. d (2 Samuel 11:2–3)
6. Aquila (Acts 18:1–3)
7. True (1 Samuel 18:27)
8. "she gave me of the tree, and I did eat" (Genesis 3:12)
9. Trick. She was given to his best man (Judges 14:20)
10. good thing (Proverbs 18:22)

QUIZ 33: I AM

1. Moses (Exodus 3:14)
2. "no man cometh unto the Father, but by me" (John 14:6)
3. jealous (Deuteronomy 5:9)
4. "the bread of life" (John 6:35)
5. c (John 8)
6. b (Matthew 3:17; 17:5)
7. "Jesus whom thou persecutest" (Acts 9:5)
8. Abraham, Isaac, Jacob (Exodus 3:6)
9. d (Revelation 1:11)
10. door (John 10:7)

QUIZ 34: IMPRISONED!

1. d (Genesis 37:28)
2. "sang praises unto God" (Acts 16:25)
3. True (Jeremiah 38:6)
4. b (Matthew 14:3–4)
5. True (Judges 16:21)
6. c (1 Kings 22:26–28)
7. Patmos (Revelation 1:9)
8. c (Acts 12)
9. True (Ephesians 3:1; Philemon 1)
10. "ye have done it unto me" (Matthew 25:40)

QUIZ 35: IN THE (BIBLE) KITCHEN

1. True (Joshua 5:10–12)
2. Andrew (John 6:5–9)
3. Trick. Jesus gave it to Judas Iscariot (John 13:26)
4. "eat, and be merry" (Luke 15:23)
5. d (Numbers 11:5)

6. Trick. They went to Egypt to purchase corn (Genesis 42:1)
7. "and hatred therewith" (Proverbs 15:17)
8. Trick. He added meal (flour) to neutralize the poison (2 Kings 4:38–41)
9. a (1 Samuel 2:12)
10. "his birthright" (Genesis 25:34)

QUIZ 36: ISRAEL AND ISRAELITES

1. d (Hosea 1:2)
2. Trick. They said, "Wherein hast thou loved us?" (Malachi 1:2)
3. Trick. They had only been in the wilderness for three days (Exodus 15:22–24)
4. c (Genesis 35:22–26)
5. Trick. There were only three—Saul, David, and Solomon, before Solomon's son Rehoboam caused the split (1 Kings 12)
6. "thou art mine" (Isaiah 43:1)
7. d (Genesis 41:56)
8. True (Exodus 14:21–22)
9. Ephraim, Manasseh (Genesis 48:19–20)
10. a (Philippians 3:4–5)

QUIZ 37: JEWELS AND JEWELRY

1. twelve (Revelation 21:21)
2. c (Exodus 39:6–7)
3. Trick. Aaron used earrings (Exodus 32:2–4)
4. "of great price" (Matthew 13:45–46)
5. rubies (Proverbs 31:10)
6. c (Genesis 24:22)
7. Trick. They gave everything to the Lord (Numbers 31:48–50)
8. d (Revelation 21:19–20)
9. knowledge (Proverbs 20:15)
10. d (James 2:1–4)

QUIZ 38: JOB'S SAD STORY

1. d (Job 1:2)
2. "Doth Job fear God for nought?" (Job 1:8–9)
3. True (Job 1:14–17)
4. seven (Job 2:13)
5. d (Job 2:11)
6. True (Job 32:1)
7. "when I laid the foundations of the earth?" (Job 38:4)
8. d (Job 42:7)
9. Trick. Job had another ten children (Job 42:13)

10. "more than his beginning" (Job 42:12)

QUIZ 39: JOSHUA FIT THE BATTLE OF JERICHO

1. True (Joshua 3:14–17)
2. "captain of the host of the LORD am I now come" (Joshua 5:13–14)
3. Trick. Priests with trumpets went first (Joshua 6:6)
4. c (Joshua 5:10)
5. "none went out, and none came in" (Joshua 6:1)
6. Trick. They marched for seven days (Joshua 6:4)
7. circumcising (Joshua 5:2–5)
8. Trick. Rahab and all that were in her house were saved (Joshua 6:17)
9. "shout with a great shout" (Joshua 6:5)
10. d (Joshua 7:1)

QUIZ 40: KINGS AND QUEENS

1. Trick. Saul was the first king of Israel (1 Samuel 10:20–24)
2. True (Esther 1:3, 9)
3. c (Judges 3:17)
4. Elijah (2 Kings 9:36)
5. a (1 Kings 10:1)
6. "tetrarch of Galilee" (Luke 3:1)
7. c (1 Kings 13:4)
8. Trick. He was seven (2 Kings 11:1–4)
9. Candace (Acts 8:27)
10. "he removeth kings, and setteth up kings" (Daniel 2:21)

QUIZ 41: KNIVES AND OTHER WEAPONS

1. c (Genesis 21:20)
2. David, Jonathan (1 Samuel 20:18–22)
3. d (Judges 20:16)
4. Trick. She did it to save the Israelites from Jabin, king of Canaan (Judges 4:2, 21)
5. d (Judges 15:16)
6. True (Numbers 25:6–8)
7. trumpets, pitchers with lamps inside (Judges 7:16)
8. c (1 Samuel 17:40)
9. d (1 Samuel 17:50–51)
10. "the word of God" (Ephesians 6:17)

QUIZ 42: "KNOW" THIS

1. "the truth shall make you free" (John 8:32)
2. "that I am God" (Psalm 46:10)

3. a (Proverbs 1:2)
4. Trick. God said He knew Jeremiah before he was in the womb (Jeremiah 1:5)
5. "Am I my brother's keeper?" (Genesis 4:9)
6. Joseph (Exodus 1:8)
7. c (Luke 23:34)
8. True (Matthew 6:31–32)
9. a (Matthew 7:15–16)
10. "if ye have love one to another" (John 13:35)

QUIZ 43: LANGUAGE ARTS

1. d (Genesis 11:6–7)
2. heavens, firmament (Psalm 19:1, 3)
3. c (Isaiah 36:11)
4. True (Nehemiah 13:24–25)
5. Trick. Every people group had its own language (Esther 8:9)
6. "Jesus of Nazareth the King of the Jews" (John 19:19–20)
7. True (Judges 12:5–6)
8. Israel (Ezekiel 3:5)
9. c (Daniel 6:25–26)
10. "full of new wine" (or drunk) (Acts 2:13)

QUIZ 44: LEADERSHIP 101

1. a (Judges 3:9)
2. True (Ezra 7:11–13)
3. cupbearer (Nehemiah 1:11)
4. "we will serve the Lord" (Joshua 24:15)
5. b (Genesis 37:22)
6. True (Galatians 2:11–16)
7. priesthood (Numbers 25:12–13)
8. Trick. It was Philip the evangelist (Acts 8:4–8)
9. Syria (2 Kings 5:1)
10. Haman (Esther 3:1)

QUIZ 45: LIES AND CONSEQUENCES

1. c (2 Kings 5:27)
2. "Ye shall not surely die" (Genesis 3:4)
3. death (Acts 5:4–5; 9–10)
4. True (1 Kings 22:22)
5. c (Genesis 39:19–20)
6. True (Genesis 37:31–34)
7. b (Daniel 2:13)
8. True (Esther 7:9)

9. d (1 Samuel 15:13–14)

10. "the man" (Matthew 26:74)

QUIZ 46: THE LIFE OF CHRIST

1. Trick. In addition to the death of Lazarus (John 11:35), Jesus also wept over Jerusalem (Luke 19:41).

2. c (Luke 4:29)

3. Trick (John 4:2)

4. "command fire to come down from heaven, and consume them" (Luke 9:54)

5. c (Tamar, Rahab, Ruth, she who was Uriah's wife [Bathsheba], and Mary)

6. "for he hath been dead four days" (John 11:39)

7. Pilate (Matthew 27:19)

8. True (Luke 9:1–2)

9. True (Matthew 26:26–30)

10. a (John 11:1)

QUIZ 47: MED CENTER

1. True (Luke 4:23)

2. Luke (Colossians 4:14)

3. "arise with healing in his wings" (Malachi 4:2)

4. d (Deuteronomy 7:12–15)

5. True (2 Kings 20:7)

6. b (Genesis 50:2)

7. c (2 Chronicles 16:12)

8. True (Job 13:4)

9. d (Revelation 3:14, 18)

10. True (Mark 8:22–26)

QUIZ 48: MIGHTY MEN

1. d (Judges 6:11–12)

2. True (1 Samuel 16:18)

3. b (1 Samuel 17:7)

4. True (Judges 16:2–3)

5. True (Joshua 14:10; 15:14)

6. d (2 Samuel 1:17–19)

7. c (1 Samuel 14:14)

8. d (2 Samuel 21:19, 1 Chronicles 11:22, 2 Samuel 23:15–16)

9. Nimrod (Genesis 10:8–9)

10. c (Judges 3:31)

QUIZ 49: MIRACLES OF JESUS

1. c (John 11:43; Luke 7:11–15; 8:53–56)
2. John (John 5:1–9)
3. "be still" (Mark 4:39)
4. d (Matthew 12:10–14)
5. True (Matthew 14:14–21; 15:32–38)
6. turning water into wine (John 2:1–11)
7. b (John 21: 1–6)
8. b (Matthew 17:24–27)
9. d (Matthew 17:15–16)
10. ear (Luke 22:50–51)

QUIZ 50: MIRACLES OF OTHER FOLKS

1. Enoch, Elijah (Genesis 5:24; 2 Kings 2:1, 11)
2. True (2 Kings 20:10–11)
3. d (Joshua 10:12–13)
4. Trick. Elisha did that (2 Kings 4:38–44)
5. d (Acts 13:9–11)
6. b (Exodus 3:1)
7. Trick. He fell upon Elisha's bones (2 Kings 13:21)
8. c (2 Kings 2:8, 14)
9. seven (2 Kings 5:14)
10. Trick. The serpent was made of brass (Numbers 21:8–9)

QUIZ 51: MONEY, MONEY, MONEY

1. "is the root of all evil" (1 Timothy 6:10)
2. Trick. Judas betrayed Jesus for thirty pieces of silver (Matthew 26:15)
3. "Caesar the things that are Caesar's, and to God the things that are God's" (Mark 12:17)
4. Trick. His money was taken and given to another man who'd increased his money tenfold (Luke 19:12–27)
5. "servant" (Proverbs 22:7)
6. d (Luke 21:1–4)
7. twenty (Genesis 37:28)
8. Trick. It was a day's wage (Matthew 20:2)
9. "and slothful servant" (Matthew 25:26)
10. Trick. Instead of a bracelet, it was an earring (Job 42:11)

QUIZ 52: NOAH AND HIS ARK

1. Trick. Methuselah was Noah's grandfather (Genesis 5:25, 28–29)
2. raven, dove (Genesis 8:7–8)

3. gopher, or cypress (Genesis 6:14)
4. Trick. Seven pairs of each "clean" animal were taken on the ark (Genesis 7:2)
5. c (Genesis 7:6)
6. eight (Genesis 7:13)
7. "shut him in" (Genesis 7:16)
8. True (1 Peter 3:20–21)
9. c (Matthew 24:37)
10. True (Genesis 7:11; 8:14)

QUIZ 53: NONE LIKE GOD

1. c (God was speaking through Moses; Exodus 9:14)
2. Trick. Not even Moses could enter (Exodus 40:35)
3. d (1 Kings 19:11–12)
4. True (Hebrews 1:1–3)
5. b (1 Samuel 2:1–2)
6. "to conceal a thing" (Proverbs 25:2)
7. Philip (John 14:9)
8. True (Malachi 1:2–3)
9. Spirits (Revelation 4:5)
10. "for God took him" (Genesis 5:24)

QUIZ 54: NORTH, SOUTH, EAST, WEST

1. "stood over where the young child was" (Matthew 2:9)
2. Trick. He spent more time in the north (Matthew 21:11)
3. vision (Acts 16:9)
4. c (Zechariah 14:4)
5. d (Genesis 28:14)
6. "Abraham, and Isaac, and Jacob, in the kingdom of heaven" (Matthew 8:11)
7. east (Genesis 3:24)
8. Trick. There are three on each wall (Revelation 21:12–13)
9. a (Numbers 34:1–3)
10. "the coming of the Son of man be" (Matthew 24:27)

QUIZ 55: O-B-E-D-I-E-N-C-E

1. d (Judges 4:9)
2. "to obey God rather than men" (Acts 5:29)
3. c (Daniel 3:10–11; 17–18)
4. sacrifice (1 Samuel 15:22)
5. "be it unto me according to thy word" (Luke 1:38)
6. d (Esther 4:16)
7. True (Daniel 6:10)

8. Moriah (Genesis 22:2)
9. "your own salvation with fear and trembling" (Philippians 2:12)
10. blessings (Deuteronomy 28:2)

QUIZ 56: OLD FOLKS
1. 969 (Genesis 5:27)
2. Trick. She was eighty-four (Luke 2:37)
3. "stricken in age" (Joshua 23:1–2)
4. c (Genesis 23:1)
5. c (Daniel 7:9)
6. five hundred (Genesis 5:32)
7. c (Deuteronomy 34:7)
8. True. He lived 930 years (Genesis 5:5)
9. "hoary head" (Leviticus 19:32)
10. Trick. Enoch lived on earth 365 years but he didn't die—God took him (Genesis 5:23–24)

QUIZ 57: OLIVES
1. d (Exodus 30:22–25)
2. "in her mouth was an olive leaf" (Genesis 8:11)
3. True (Luke 22:39; Mark 14:32)
4. continually (Leviticus 24:2)
5. d (Zechariah 14:4)
6. Trick. She brought gold, precious stones, and spices (1 Kings 10:10)
7. a (Psalm 128:3)
8. Gentile believers (Romans 11:13, 17)
9. Trick. The Bible doesn't name the mountain, though some scholars suggest it was Mount Tabor (Matthew 17:1–9)
10. "but thou shalt not anoint thee with oil" (Micah 6:15)

QUIZ 58: PEOPLE TO SEE
1. d (Genesis 12, 26)
2. c (2 Samuel 14:25–26)
3. tender eyed (Genesis 29:17)
4. Trick. Just try to find it!
5. Vashti (Esther 1:10–12)
6. "the daughters of Job" (Job 42:15)
7. Bathsheba (2 Samuel 11:2–3)
8. b (Song of Solomon 7:1–7)
9. Nabal (1 Samuel 25)
10. "a meek and quiet spirit" (1 Peter 3:1–4)

QUIZ 59: PLACES TO BE

1. Endor (1 Samuel 28:7)
2. True—over the tribe of Judah (2 Samuel 2:1–4)
3. d (Joshua 10:1)
4. True (Luke 10:30)
5. "whose goings forth have been from of old, from everlasting" (Micah 5:2)
6. Samaria (John 4:5–7)
7. c (Judges 18:31; 1 Samuel 4:3)
8. Babel (Genesis 11:9)
9. Trick. Moses saw the promised land from Mount Nebo (Deuteronomy 34:1)
10. c (Jeremiah 43:7–8)

QUIZ 60: PLAY ME A SONG

1. True (Exodus 15:1; Revelation 15:3)
2. d (Numbers 21:17)
3. Miriam (Exodus 15:21)
4. True (Book of Psalms)
5. a (Ecclesiastes 7:5)
6. True (1 Samuel 18:7–9)
7. "in my mouth" (Psalm 40:3)
8. a (Proverbs 25:20)
9. "in your heart to the Lord" (Ephesians 5:19)
10. a (Job 35:10)

QUIZ 61: PROPHETS AND PROPHECIES

1. d (Isaiah 8:3)
2. "I come quickly" (Revelation 22:20)
3. John the Baptist (Luke 7:28)
4. Moses, Elijah (Matthew 17:3)
5. True (Revelation 2:20)
6. c (Ezekiel 48:35)
7. True (Exodus 15:20)
8. Isaiah (Isaiah 7:14)
9. True (1 Samuel 10:9–12)
10. "his heel" (Genesis 3:15)

QUIZ 62: QUAILS AND OTHER FOWL

1. True (Leviticus 11:13–18)
2. Peter (Mark 14:29–30)
3. Trick. Jesus Himself made one such reference (Matthew 23:37)
4. raven (Genesis 8:7)

5. "your heavenly Father feedeth them" (Matthew 6:26)
6. ravens (1 Kings 17:4)
7. "descending like a dove, and lighting upon him" (Matthew 3:16)
8. c (Luke 12:6)
9. d (Leviticus 11:16–19)
10. eagles (Isaiah 40:31)

QUIZ 63: RABBI! RABBI!

1. c (Luke 10:25–37)
2. Trick. It was the rich young ruler who asked this
   (Mark 10:17–22)
3. c (John 1:35–38)
4. c (Matthew 19:3)
5. "is not yet come" (John 2:1–4)
6. "whom thou persecutest" (Acts 9:5)
7. a (Mark 5:2–7)
8. Trick. Their eyes were opened after He broke bread for them
   (Luke 24:13–31)
9. Jonah (Matthew 16:1–4)
10. Simon Peter (Matthew 16:15–16)

QUIZ 64: REDEEMED, HOW I LOVE TO PROCLAIM IT

1. c (Mark 5:25–34)
2. eunuch (Acts 8:37–38)
3. Trick. Peter told Cornelius about Jesus (Acts 10)
4. c (Luke 19:1–9)
5. True (Ruth 4:1–8)
6. True. If a person had the means, he could even redeem himself
   (Leviticus 25:47–55)
7. "at the latter day upon the earth" (Job 19:25)
8. blood (Colossians 1:14)
9. "because the days are evil" (Ephesians 5:16)
10. eternal (Hebrews 9:12)

QUIZ 65: RICHES, FALSE AND TRUE

1. Trick. The Gospel writers Matthew (6:24) and Luke (16:13) did
2. "thieves do not break through nor steal" (Matthew 6:20)
3. True (1 Kings 10:21)
4. "Who then can be saved?" (Matthew 19:25)
5. True (Proverbs 23:5)
6. Trick. He went away sad because of his great wealth
   (Luke 18:18–23)
7. a (Ephesians 3:8)

8. b (Luke 12:20)
9. d (Revelation 3:14–18)
10. Trick. God gave Job twice as much (Job 42:10)

QUIZ 66: THE RESURRECTION
1. Martha (John 11:24–25)
2. "roll us away the stone from the door of the sepulchre?" (Mark 16:3)
3. Trick. There was an earthquake (Matthew 28:2)
4. living, dead (Luke 24:5)
5. b (John 20:6–7)
6. "they believed them not" (Luke 24:10–11)
7. d (Matthew 28:12)
8. True (John 20:19)
9. Trick. It was "Doubting" Thomas (John 20:24–25)
10. c (Luke 24:50–53)

QUIZ 67: SAYINGS OF JESUS
1. "Lot's wife" (Luke 17:32)
2. True (Mark 6:4)
3. d (John 13:26–27)
4. "and unto God the things that are God's" (Matthew 22:21)
5. Lazarus (John 11:14, 34)
6. d (John 20:1–15)
7. "Feed my sheep" (John 21:15–17)
8. John (Revelation 1:8–9)
9. b (Mark 12:18–24)
10. True (Matthew 24:14)

QUIZ 68: SCRIPTURE ON SCRIPTURE
1. "for instruction in righteousness" (2 Timothy 3:16)
2. d (Isaiah 55:11)
3. d (Daniel 10:21)
4. "sin against thee" (Psalm 119:11)
5. True (2 Timothy 3:15)
6. two-edged sword (Hebrews 4:12)
7. "the sword of the Spirit" (Ephesians 6:17)
8. c (Psalm 119:89)
9. True (Revelation 19:11–16)
10. b (John 5:39)

QUIZ 69: SERVANTS ALL
1. b (Ecclesiastes 12:13)
2. robbery (Philippians 2:6–7)

3. "that was set before him" (Hebrews 12:2)

4. c (Romans 12:1)

5. "must be about my Father's business?" (Luke 2:49)

6. d (Proverbs 3:27)

7. "nor the servant above his lord" (Matthew 10:24)

8. a (Revelation 2:18–19)

9. presumptuous (Psalm 19:13)

10. "shall serve him" (Revelation 22:3)

QUIZ 70: SHADOW OF DEATH

1. "of his saints" (Psalm 116:15)

2. 23 (verse 4)

3. Trick. It was the Lord who passed over (Exodus 12:23)

4. "but the end thereof are the ways of death" (Proverbs 14:12)

5. d (Revelation 20:14)

6. True (John 21:18–19)

7. c (2 Kings 20:1–6)

8. True (Genesis 25:9–10)

9. three (Luke 23:44)

10. "where is thy victory?" (1 Corinthians 15:55)

QUIZ 71: SHEEP AND THE SHEPHERD

1. goats (Matthew 25:31–33)

2. "his life for the sheep" (John 10:11)

3. d (Psalm 100:3)

4. great (Hebrews 13:20)

5. True (John 10:3)

6. c (John 10:7)

7. Trick. He only told one (Matthew 18:10–14)

8. Trick. He leads us for His name's sake (Psalm 23:3)

9. a (1 Peter 5:4)

10. "taketh away the sin of the world" (John 1:29)

QUIZ 72: SIMON PETER

1. Joel (Acts 2:16)

2. d (Matthew 17:4)

3. Trick. It was the other way around (John 20:1–7)

4. c (Matthew 14:22–33)

5. True (Acts 12:4)

6. three (John 21:15–17)

7. Trick. Peter was sleeping (Matthew 26:40)

8. two (1 and 2 Peter). But many believe he was a primary source for Mark's Gospel as well.

9. Trick. There was also Simon the Canaanite (Mark 3:14–19)

10. c (Matthew 8:14–15)

QUIZ 73: SIN, UGH

1. "eternal life through Jesus Christ our Lord" (Romans 6:23)

2. abomination (Proverbs 6:16–19)

3. Trick. It was Ananias and his wife, Sapphira (Acts 5:1–10)

4. Sodom, Gomorrah (Genesis 19:24)

5. c (Numbers 31:1–8)

6. "to him it is sin" (James 4:17)

7. b (Numbers 12)

8. b (Psalm 103:12)

9. "to cleanse us from all unrighteousness" (1 John 1:9)

10. True (Ephesians 4:26)

QUIZ 74: SOLDIERY

1. c (Isaiah 37:36–37)

2. Trick. David fought the Philistines to marry Michal
   (1 Samuel 18:25–29)

3. Ezra (Ezra 8:22)

4. d (2 Chronicles 20:18–23)

5. three hundred (Judges 7:3, 6)

6. "in the name of the LORD of hosts" (1 Samuel 17:45)

7. True (2 Kings 6:15–17)

8. d (1 Samuel 5–6)

9. b (1 Samuel 29:9)

10. weapon (Nehemiah 4:17)

QUIZ 75: SOLOMON SAYS

1. vanity, vanities, vanity (Ecclesiastes 1:2)

2. True, if not in so many words (Ecclesiastes 10:20)

3. b (Ecclesiastes 10:1)

4. "the beginning of knowledge" (Proverbs 1:7)

5. Trick. "Pride goeth before destruction, and an haughty spirit
   before a fall" (Proverbs 16:18)

6. True (Proverbs 6:27)

7. d (Ecclesiastes 4:9–11)

8. love (Song of Solomon 8:7)

9. "and he shall direct thy paths" (Proverbs 3:5–6)

10. c (Proverbs 16:7)

QUIZ 76: SOWING, REAPING

1. c (Matthew 6:26)

2. corruption, life everlasting (Galatians 6:8)

3. True (Hosea 8:7)
4. six (Leviticus 25:3)
5. d (Leviticus 25:11)
6. tears, joy (Psalm 126:5)
7. vanity (Proverbs 22:8)
8. b (Psalm 97:11)
9. wind, clouds (Ecclesiastes 11:4)
10. "and he which soweth bountifully shall reap also bountifully" (2 Corinthians 9:6)

QUIZ 77: SUFFERING'S BRIGHT SIDE

1. "I will be with thee" (Isaiah 43:2)
2. d (Revelation 2:1, 7)
3. "meant it unto good" (Genesis 50:20)
4. "uphold thee with the right hand of my righteousness" (Isaiah 41:10)
5. righteousness' (1 Peter 3:14)
6. d (Genesis 49:22–25)
7. d (Psalm 23:4)
8. forsaken (2 Corinthians 4:9)
9. "what man shall do unto me" (Hebrews 13:6)
10. Trick. It is renewed day by day (2 Corinthians 4:16)

QUIZ 78: TABERNACLE AND TEMPLE

1. c (Exodus 35:30–35)
2. "and the glory of the Lord filled the tabernacle" (Exodus 40:34)
3. ark of the covenant (Exodus 40:1–7)
4. Levi (Numbers 3:17–37)
5. b (Exodus 30:23–29)
6. True (1 Chronicles 17:1–4)
7. Trick. After the Babylonian captivity, Zerubbabel built a temple in Jerusalem (Zechariah 4:9)
8. "endureth for ever" (2 Chronicles 7:3)
9. d (John 2:20)
10. d (Revelation 11:19)

QUIZ 79: TAXED ENOUGH ALREADY

1. Matthew (Matthew 9:9–13)
2. True (Luke 2:1–5)
3. Egypt (2 Kings 23:34–35)
4. Trick. The short, rich tax collector of Jericho was Zacchaeus (Luke 19:1–2)

5. True (Matthew 17:24–27)

6. a (Ezra 4:7–13)

7. Trick. It was a Pharisee (Luke 18:9–14)

8. "to give tribute to Caesar, or not?" (Mark 12:14–17)

9. True (Nehemiah 5:4)

10. Trick. It was the Ephraimites (Joshua 16:5–10)

QUIZ 80: TEN COMMANDMENTS

1. True. In Matthew 22:38, Jesus was quoting Deuteronomy 6:5.

2. (1) Thou shalt have no other gods before me. (2) Thou shall not make unto thee any graven image. (3) Thou shalt not take the name of the Lord thy God in vain. (4) Remember the sabbath day to keep it holy. (5) Honour thy father and thy mother.

3. (6) Thou shalt not kill. (7) Thou shalt not commit adultery. (8) Thou shalt not steal. (9) Thou shalt not bear false witness against thy neighbour. (10) Thou shalt not covet. . .any thing that is thy neighbour's.

4. b (Ephesians 6:2–3)

5. a (Exodus 31:18)

6. forty (Deuteronomy 9:9)

7. b (Exodus 24:13–14)

8. "out of the land of Egypt, out of the house of bondage" (Exodus 20:2)

9. rested (Exodus 20:11)

10. Trick. That appears to be Jesus' summary of the final six commandments (Mark 12:31)

QUIZ 81: THANK YOU! THANK YOU!

1. d (Luke 17:11–19)

2. a (2 Kings 5:15)

3. Mary, the mother of Jesus (Luke 1:46–47)

4. Trick. Paul said to give thanks "in every thing" (1 Thessalonians 5:18)

5. thanksgiving, praise (Psalm 100:4)

6. c (Philippians 1:3)

7. True (Nehemiah 12:8)

8. "I must abide at thy house" (Luke 19:5–6)

9. c (Philippians 4:11)

10. "through Jesus Christ our Lord" (Romans 7:24–25)

QUIZ 82: THEFT

1. c (Joshua 7:20–21)

2. Trick. Naaman was a leper (2 Kings 5:22, 27)

3. True (Genesis 31:30)

4. tithes (Malachi 3:8–9)

5. Rebekah, their mother (Genesis 27)

6. "made it a den of thieves" (Matthew 21:12–13)

7. "steal, and to kill, and to destroy" (John 10:10)

8. b (Proverbs 6:30)

9. a (John 10:1)

10. "be with me in paradise" (Luke 23:40–43)

QUIZ 83: THE TRINITY

1. "in our image" (Genesis 1:26)

2. transfiguration (Matthew 17:1–5)

3. d (John 14:17, 26)

4. b (John 10:30–31)

5. "the Word was God" (John 1:1)

6. "express image of his person" (Hebrews 1:1–3)

7. Trick. The Spirit of God moved upon the face of the waters (Genesis 1:2)

8. witnesses (Acts 1:8)

9. a (2 Corinthians 13:14)

10. Father, Son, Holy Ghost (Matthew 28:19–20)

QUIZ 84: TROUBLOUS TIMES

1. d (1 Kings 16:33–17:1)

2. True (2 Chronicles 36:1–7)

3. b (2 Kings 17:1–6)

4. famine (Ruth 1:1)

5. "these are the beginnings of sorrows" (Mark 13:8)

6. b (Exodus 7:19–25)

7. True (2 Kings 6:24–25)

8. 185,000 (2 Kings 19:32–35)

9. Purim (Esther 9:26)

10. Death, Hell (Revelation 6:7–8)

QUIZ 85: TWELVE (OR SO) DISCIPLES

1. Trick. It was Peter's brother, Andrew (John 1:35–40)

2. Matthias (Acts 1:26)

3. True (Luke 8:3)

4. "let the dead bury their dead" (Matthew 8:21–22)

5. c (Acts 9:27)

6. one, four (John 19:25–26)

7. "for fear of the Jews" (John 19:38)

8. c (Luke 10:1)

9. Antioch (Acts 11:26)
10. Trick. He called himself the *least* of the apostles
    (1 Corinthians 15:9)

QUIZ 86: THE "UN"-COLA

1. unawares (Hebrews 13:2)
2. Trick. He needed to bring a trespass offering (Leviticus 5:2–6)
3. understanding (Proverbs 9:10)
4. "a breaker of the law" (Romans 2:25)
5. "help thou mine unbelief" (Mark 9:23–24)
6. undefiled (James 1:27)
7. c (1 Timothy 6:14)
8. d (Psalm 145:3)
9. unpunished (Proverbs 19:5)
10. a (Luke 6:35–36)

QUIZ 87: UP IN THE SKY

1. knowledge (Psalm 19:1–2)
2. True (Matthew 24:30)
3. True (Matthew 16:2–3)
4. c (Numbers 24:15–17)
5. b (Job 38:4–7)
6. fourth (Genesis 1:14–19)
7. "are come to worship him" (Matthew 2:2)
8. True (2 Kings 23:5)
9. c (2 Kings 20:10)
10. "which may be felt" (Exodus 10:21)

QUIZ 88: VIGILANCE

1. c (Esther 2:7)
2. bridegroom (Matthew 25:1–13)
3. "keeping watch over their flock by night" (Luke 2:8)
4. c (1 Thessalonians 5:6)
5. True (1 Samuel 19:10–12)
6. "that your labour is not in vain in the Lord"
   (1 Corinthians 15:58)
7. a (Galatians 6:9)
8. c (1 Timothy 3:2)
9. "sin lieth at the door" (Genesis 4:7)
10. lead, hold (Psalm 139:9–10)

QUIZ 89: VILLAINS AND TROUBLEMAKERS

1. Haman (Esther 7:6)
2. Ahab, Jezebel (1 Kings 16:29–31)

3. c (Numbers 16:30)
4. True. His bed was nine cubits, or about fourteen feet, long (Deuteronomy 3:11)
5. d. But he was actually hoping to come back later and rescue Joseph, whom the other brothers wanted to kill (Genesis 37:22)
6. c (Genesis 37:26–27)
7. Trick. It was the presidents and princes who tricked the king (Daniel 6:6–7)
8. c (2 Timothy 3:8)
9. True (1 John 2:18, 22, 4:3; 2 John 7)
10. "they had killed Paul" (Acts 23:12)

QUIZ 90: THE VIRGIN BIRTH

1. Isaiah (Isaiah 7:14)
2. c (Micah 5:2)
3. "two years old and under" (Matthew 2:16)
4. Trick. The Bible only says they were "in the same country" (Luke 2:8)
5. eight (Luke 2:21)
6. c (Luke 2:24)
7. Trick. The angel told them to flee to Egypt (Matthew 2:13)
8. "Ye shall find the babe wrapped in swaddling clothes, lying in a manger" (Luke 2:12)
9. d (Luke 2:1)
10. "there was no room for them in the inn" (Luke 2:7)

QUIZ 91: WARS AND RUMORS OF WARS

1. b (Genesis 14)
2. True (Revelation 19–20)
3. b. They were heirs of his second wife, Keturah (Genesis 25:1–2)
4. Trick. The Israelites couldn't cut down any fruit or nut-bearing trees (Deuteronomy 20:19–20)
5. Philistines (1 Samuel 9:15–17)
6. Nebuchadnezzar, Babylon (Jeremiah 21:1–4)
7. Trick. Moses called God "a man of war" (Exodus 15:3)
8. "all their days" (1 Kings 14:30)
9. d (Deuteronomy 20:1–9)
10. "learn war any more" (Micah 4:3)

QUIZ 92: WATER LINES

1. Trick. He told a Samaritan woman at a well (John 4:10)
2. Elisha (2 Kings 3)

3. "after many days" (Ecclesiastes 11:1)
4. thirsty, ground (Isaiah 44:3)
5. True (Matthew 5:45)
6. "and seek my face, and turn from their wicked ways"
   (2 Chronicles 7:14)
7. d (2 Kings 2:8, 14)
8. True (Exodus 14:21–22)
9. repentance (Matthew 3:11)
10. sea (Revelation 21:1)

QUIZ 93: WISDOM AND FOLLY
1. True. Guess it depends on the fool. . . (Proverbs 26:4–5)
2. "and great was the fall of it" (Matthew 7:26–27)
3. "apply our hearts unto wisdom" (Psalm 90:12)
4. True (Luke 12:19)
5. d (Ecclesiastes 9:18)
6. c (Job 39:26)
7. wives (1 Kings 11:4)
8. d (James 3:17)
9. "that giveth to all men liberally, and upbraideth not"
   (James 1:5)
10. "There is no God" (Psalm 14:1)

QUIZ 94: WOMEN FOLK
1. True (Exodus 4:24–26)
2. Grecian, or Greek (Acts 6:1)
3. d (Hebrews 11:11; 31)
4. Trick. She's there, but she is not mentioned by name
   (Matthew 1:6)
5. c (Acts 8:27)
6. Trick. It was the daughters of Zelophehad (Numbers 27:6–8)
7. c (Judges 4:21–22)
8. Elisha (2 Kings 4:8)
9. Trick. A dragon pursued the woman (Revelation 12:4–9)
10. c (Genesis 16:1)

QUIZ 95: X MARKS THE SPOT
1. "sold all that he had, and bought it" (Matthew 13:45–46)
2. c (2 Chronicles 20:25)
3. gods, or idols (Genesis 31:30)
4. "there will your heart be also" (Matthew 6:21)
5. crowns (Revelation 4:10)
6. d (2 Kings 18:14–16)

7. b (Deuteronomy 28:12)

8. "trouble therewith" (Proverbs 15:16)

9. a (Hebrews 11:24–26)

10. gold, frankincense, myrrh (Matthew 2:11)

QUIZ 96: YEARNINGS

1. "all these things shall be added unto you" (Matthew 6:33)

2. True (1 Kings 10:1)

3. eternal life (Luke 18:18)

4. True (Genesis 24:1–4)

5. Macedonia (Acts 16:9)

6. fourteen (Genesis 29:15–30)

7. d (Psalm 19:10)

8. nations (Haggai 2:7)

9. d (Genesis 43:29–30)

10. True (Psalm 27:4)

QUIZ 97: YOUTH GROUP

1. twelve (Luke 2:42–47)

2. "five barley loaves, and two small fishes" (John 6:9)

3. c (1 Samuel 16:11)

4. "I drew him out of the water" (Exodus 2:10)

5. c (2 Kings 5:2)

6. lamb (Genesis 22:7)

7. c (1 Samuel 3:3–4)

8. "he will not depart from it" (Proverbs 22:6)

9. True (Acts 20:9)

10. Trick. Rachel was the mother of Jacob's youngest son (Genesis 35:18)

QUIZ 98: "Z" PEOPLE

1. Trick. Zephaniah is the thirty-sixth book of the Old Testament; Zechariah is the thirty-eighth.

2. a (Genesis 30:19–20)

3. True (Genesis 29:24)

4. David (1 Chronicles 24:3, 31)

5. b (Esther 5:10)

6. James, John (Matthew 4:21)

7. Trick. He was the final king of Judah (2 Chronicles 36:10)

8. governor (Haggai 1:1)

9. a (Genesis 25:1–2)

10. b (1 Kings 16:15)